Praise for *Whatever You Do, Don't Run:*

"Allison's infectious enthusiasm for both the African bush and his job showing its wonders to tourists is readily apparent." —*Booklist*

"His misadventures make *Whatever You Do, Don't Run* an absorbing read. . . . The material is rich, and Allison is a gifted storyteller. And the only thing stranger than African fiction is African truth." —*National Geographic Adventure*

"After reading this entrancing memoir, an African safari may move to No. 1 on your travel wish list. The only catch is you'll want the author as your guide." —*Chicago Sun-Times*

Praise for *Don't Look Behind You!:*

"The best compliment you can pay a travel writer is to read his work and feel like you're right there with him. For more than two hundred pages, I felt like I was in Africa, up to my neck in danger. I don't even know this guy, but more than once I lay awake at night, worrying for his safety. Enough adventure, action, life lessons, and laughs to fill a movie and four sequels. The fact that Allison survived to write any of this down is a miracle in itself." —Cash Peters, author of *Naked in Dangerous Places and Gullible's Travels*

How to Walk a Puma

AND OTHER THINGS I LEARNED WHILE STUMBLING THROUGH SOUTH AMERICA

Peter Allison

LYONS PRESS
Guilford, Connecticut
An imprint of Globe Pequot Press

Lyons Press is an imprint of Globe Pequot Press.

Project editor: David Legere
Text design: Lisa Reneson
Layout artist: Sue Murray

Library of Congress Cataloging-in-Publication Data

Allison, Peter.
  How to walk a puma : and other things I learned while stumbling through South America / Peter Allison.
    p. cm.
  ISBN 978-0-7627-7756-3
  1. Allison, Peter—Travel—Patagonia (Argentina and Chile) 2. Patagonia (Argentina and Chile)—Description and travel. I. Title.
  G156.A44 2012
  918.2'704411092—dc23

2011038618

Printed in the United States of America

10 9 8 7 6 5 4 3 2 1

This is a book about escaping a desk, hitting the road, and collecting new experiences. While this is an exciting thing to do, there is always the downside of leaving treasured people behind. In my case it is my wonderful sister Laurie and my niece and nephew, Molly and Riley Taylor, plus my friends Nick Goodwin, Hayden Jones, and Marc Butler. Huge thanks must also go to the family Gomez, who looked after me so well on my arrival and on many subsequent visits. I love you all, despite the names I call you.

Contents

Acknowledgments   xi

Introduction   xvii

1 Running with Roy   1

2 Roy's Big Day Out   11

3 Don't Eat My Hero   19

4 Dressed for a Kill   25

5 The Last Temptation of Roy   33

6 Not the End of the World   39

7 The Empanada Disaster   45

8 Blue World   51

9 The Road from Patagonia   57

10 The Joy of Pessimism   69

11 There Is a Jaguar, Right Here!   79

12 8.8   85

13 Getting High in Bolivia   95

14 Take Me to the River   103

15 Puff, the Magic Canoe   121

16 One Hundred Ways to Bleed   127

17 The Idiot Box   133

18 Beekeeping in the Amazon   141

Contents

19 All You Can Eat   147

20 A Month of Monkeys, a Night of Darkness 157

21 Going Deeper   165

22 Tigre! Tigre!   173

23 Parrots, Prayers, and the End of a Year   181

24 Chasing a Jaguar   185

25 The Honeymoon Period   195

Afterword   199

About the Author   201

Acknowledgments

My sincere thanks go to the following people:

Harris and Marguerite Gomez, for giving me the softest landing imaginable in South America and being such wonderful friends.

Pete Oxford and Renee Bish, wildlife photographers extraordinaire, for saving my bacon, then putting it in some of the most exciting situations I have been in. Much of this book would not have come about without their advice and introductions. They have also produced an incredible photographic account of time they spent deep in Yasuni, titled *Spirit of the Huaorani*. If the stories here have spurred any interest in the subject, I cannot recommend this book strongly enough.

The Minke, for more than can be said or written.

Tom Quesenberry (now that's a funny name, isn't it?) and Mariela Tenorio, who run the beautiful El Monte Lodge in Mindo, for arranging and assisting with so much of the Huaorani trip, and laughing as heartily as the Huaorani at all my maladies.

Bec Smart, Bondy, Mick Payne, Adrian, Rob Thoren, Nina at Inti Wara Yassi, home of Roy the puma.

Sam Sudar, for getting in a car with me.

Julio, the night watchman at Hostel Americana in El Calafate.

Marcello Yndio, for the way he killed a chicken.

Peter Fitzsimmons, for coffee, advice—and constant reminders that he sells more books than me.

Guillerme and Andres at the Sacha office, Tomas the manager, as well as all the staff at Sacha Lodge, for making my stay there so pleasurable and monkey filled.

Aaron Sorkin, for answering so many questions, and the Undeletables, for laughs and thought-provoking debate.

Marcela Liljesthrom, for the swallows.

Friedereke "Wildchild" Wildberg, for some wise words, but mainly for being German, yet funny.

Lloyd Temple Camp, because he wants to be mentioned in a book.

Donald Brown, for the same reason (and yes, yes, yes, it is true, he also kept me employed for two years when few people would).

Tarli Young, for saving me from a planned life of luxury and comfort in Costa Rica and inadvertently sending me to Bolivia and Inti Wara Yassi instead.

Ben and Kate Loxton, for insisting I waste some time in debauchery and laugh myself silly while doing so. And Yahtzee, too.

Diana Balcazar, for expert guiding while filming in Colombia.

Matt Mitchell and Jonny Hall at Hostel Revolution, Quito.

John Purcell and Tamsin Steel, for putting me up—and putting up with me—when I was recently single and a moping dullard.

Louis, Hoens, and Jan Louis Nortje, who gave me somewhere to stay during the main editing phase of this book, far from South America in Namibia.

My wonderful agent and friend, Kate Epstein of the Epstein Literary Agency. As always she went above and beyond to make this the best book it can be.

Holly Rubino, Gail Blackhall, Nicholas Brealey, Tom Viney, Nadia Manuelli, Helen Holyoake, Joan de la Haye, Louise Thurtell, and Angela Handley for their work on this book and prior tomes as well. Special appreciation goes to the late Nick Pryke of Wild Dog Press in South Africa.

There's a race of men that don't fit in,
A race that can't stay still;
So they break the hearts of kith and kin,
And they roam the world at will.
They range the field and they rove the flood,
And they climb the mountain's crest;
Theirs is the curse of the gypsy blood,
And they don't know how to rest.

—Robert W. Service, "The Men Who Don't Fit In,"
The Spell of the Yukon and Other Verses, 1907

I was sixteen and on a scholarship for a year in Japan.

A series of near Biblical plagues overtook my host family's city of Okayama. First came praying mantises, which begat a plague of frogs that emerged en masse from the city's open drains in pursuit of the bounty of insects. Then there were the snakes.

For the townspeople this was a nightmare. I was delighted. My host family's cat was the only one to share my enthusiasm, and she caught the snakes alive and dumped them proudly at the bare feet of whichever startled member of the family was at home.

"Piitaa!" would come the cry, and I would sally from my room and perform what they saw as an act of lunacy by scooping up the snake and taking it back to the slime from which it had come.

"Sayonara," I would farewell. "*Hiss*," the snake would reply, if at all.

Three years later I decided to head overseas to somewhere that had an abundance of wildlife. I'd been to Asia, and I lived in Australia. My staple diet of documentary television told me there were really only two choices. So in late 1993, a few days before my nineteenth birthday, I used the most rigorous and scientific method I could think of to decide between South America and Africa: I tossed a coin.

Africa came up heads that day and changed my life. I thought I would stay for a year and then please my father and go to law school, but my passion for wildlife won out while I was visiting a safari camp and I was offered employment behind their bar. Over the years I worked my way up and became a safari guide, a camp manager, and ultimately a teacher for those wishing to get into the business of guiding. In that time I had some of the best experiences with animals that anyone who loves them could wish for. I witnessed an elephant giving birth, was charged by lions, had a leopard walk into my tent, and made friends with a family of cheetahs that would allow me to lie down beside them. I stayed seven years. Eventually, though, I felt I wasn't doing the job a service, tired as I was of the demands of tourists, and I also felt that all that fun somehow meant I was cheating at life. I moved back to Sydney.

I had always wondered what would have happened if the coin had landed tails that day. So in late 2009, sixteen years after the coin toss and hopefully an equivalent number of years wiser, I made my way to Santiago, Chile, ready to seek out the continent's best, weirdest, and maddest wilderness experiences. I was fresh from the breakup of a long relationship and ready to foreswear my suburban life and my tedious desk job.

I'm a firm believer that the worst decisions often lead to the best adventures, but I am no longer in my twenties. My knees are weak and my back abused. Yet South America held challenges—dense rain forests, high mountains, waterless deserts, vast and lonely steppes, as well as dangerous animals like jaguars, pumas, and bushmaster snakes—that I desperately wanted to seek out. In Africa I could have been trampled by elephants or consumed by lions. In South America the most dangerous animal is a kaleidoscopic frog so toxic that just touching it can be lethal. There is a bird in South America that evades its predators by simply being too smelly to eat. Then there are sloths, which are so slow that algae actually grow on them. I wanted to see all these animals and more, but more than any bird, fish, or reptile, I wanted to fulfill an ambition borne of all those nature documentaries I'd watched as a child: to see a wild jaguar. Armed with bad Spanish, dangerous levels of curiosity, and a record of poor judgment, my plan was to spend at least a year to find out if I could tackle whatever South America could throw at me.

So it was on September 11, 2009, that I watched every one of my possessions slide on a rubber mat toward the belly of a plane that would take me to Santiago, Chile. At the age of thirty-four I was finally going to find out what would have happened if the coin had landed tails.

Running with Roy

In Bolivia, in a patch of forest near the small town of Villa Tunari, lives a puma. His russet fur shows that he is a jungle puma (mountain pumas wear gray coats), but he wasn't born there. At the age of around six weeks he was confiscated by wildlife authorities from a marketplace. The wildlife authorities then delivered him to a group called Inti Wara Yassi—the name means "sun, stars, moon" in three separate indigenous languages—who take in such animals, care for them as best they can, and release them when possible. This particular puma has noble features, is strongly muscled, and deserves the mighty name of some Inca king. But instead he is simply called Roy. And I was tied to him for a month.

I got to know Roy while I was volunteering at Parque Machia, a small reserve where hundreds of animals live. Inti runs it and two other parks. Founded out of nothing but goodwill and run in the same way, Inti is still a young organization, held together by hope, a strong desire to do good, bananas (lots of bananas), but very little money. Parque Machia was the first stop on my quest to learn about South America's wilderness. After a flight from Santiago to crumbly old Santa Cruz, one of Bolivia's larger towns, I'd hopped onto a surprisingly modern bus. Its passengers were mainly locals, with a smattering of backpackers. Among the locals were bowler-hat-and poncho-wearing women, a sight that went from captivating to commonplace quickly as the bus ride afforded glimpses of the same style in village after village. After a day of traveling I stumbled from the bus at four in the afternoon, only halfway from Santa Cruz to the next actual town.

Parque Machia has monkeys, bears, ocelots, coatis, macaws, eagles, and pumas, but tourists mainly get to see the monkeys, which are very relaxed with humans. To reduce their stress, the majority of the animals see no one but their handlers, and while Bolivians founded and manage Parque Machia, most of the staff is made up of short-term volunteers from every corner of the globe.

My fellow new arrivals and I were waiting for an induction, something I imagined would be informal based on the ramshackle structures I had seen. Despite brightly painted murals of animals, scrawled notes of affection crumbled off concrete walls and what steel existed seemed held together by rust. Even looming powerlines, presumably not maintained by the reserve, appeared to tilt. Later in my stay I would have a new definition of suspense when a sloth started crossing these lines as a lightning storm approached—he made it, but not before a group gathered to shout encouragement and frustration at the slow-mo replay movements. Bolivia is South America's poorest country, and it's remarkable that the people who run Inti care more about animals than themselves.

The volunteers who did pass us all wore tattered clothes and had the besmirched look of refugees. "A monkey just spunked on me!" one woman exclaimed. "That's after being shat and pissed on this week already!" It probably says more about me than anything else that I actually found her quite attractive.

My first evening at Parque Machia, I joined the other new volunteers to listen to an Australian named Bondy give us a rundown on the park and to get assigned to a species of animal. The group of volunteers at Inti while I was there was made up of a close cluster of Israelis, a smattering of French, a few Americans, a disproportionate number of Australians, one or two Italians, and a lone Norwegian. (He was quite thrilled when two Danes arrived, since he could understand them.) We pieced together communication through intersecting languages and our shared love of animals. "My sort of people," I thought.

Bondy spoke of monkeys, macaws, less familiar creatures like tayra and coatis, and finally, the cats. "You have to be fit to work with Roy," said Bondy. "He covers a lot of ground each session, most of it at a run, over rough terrain that can snap an ankle or smash knees. He nails the guys with him all the time so they never get any rest. And when I say 'nail' I mean that he grabs the back of your legs with his paws then bites you on the knee. So you have to be fit—fit and a little bit crazy."

That, I thought, sounds wildly irresponsible, dangerous, and maybe a bit stupid. "That," I said with hand raised, showing flagrant disregard for the weakened knees and sore back I'd developed since I arrived in Africa at nineteen, "sounds like me."

■ ■

"He gets a bit more unpredictable when there are new guys," Mick warned me the next day, as I stumbled along a trail behind him to Roy's enclosure, already feeling a burn in my thigh muscles.

Yet another Australian, Mick had been at Parque Machia for three months, well beyond the average stay for a volunteer. (When we leave our little continent, Australians tend to stay in places a long time in dread of the long flight home.) Mick had spent six weeks of his three months with Roy, and despite frequent abuse at the paws and teeth of the puma (if a bun had been placed on either side of Mick's knee, it would have made a convincing hamburger), he was clearly in love with the big cat.

"What do you mean by 'unpredictable'?" I asked.

"Well, usually he'll only run in certain places, downhill mainly, and he runs after he takes a dump. But on days like today with a new guy he might drag us around all morning. He also gets jumpier."

"Jumpy, like nervous?"

"Nah mate, jumpy like he jumps on you and bites your knee. It will happen to you, don't worry."

Don't worry? The idea of a puma jumping on me seemed a perfectly reasonable thing to worry about.

Roy was about the size of a German shepherd, though beneath his red fur he was much more conspicuously muscled than any dog. His fur was smooth to the touch and horse-like in texture. On his face the fur had patches of an impossibly brilliant white around the nose and mouth, counterpointed by eye markings of deep ebony. His facial features were surprisingly delicate—most male cats have squared-off muzzles and a certain tightness around the eyes. Roy had the softer, smoother features of a female.

I touched Roy for the first time, on his muzzle and around his silken ears, there in his pen. He accepted the pat, but with a cat's aloofness, as if the pleasure is not theirs at all. In this instance he may have been right.

I watched Mick as he clipped a rope around his waist with a sturdy carabineer, before connecting the other end of the thirty-three-foot rope to Roy's collar.

"He usually runs a bit up this first slope," Mick warned over his shoulder, his eyes sticking resolutely to Roy's muscular shoulders.

"How far he runs gives you an idea what sort of morning you will have," added Adrian, who had been training to work with Roy only a few days and was coming along with us. Adrian, who was known at the park as the "Nordic Giant" had recently completed two years' military service for the Norwegian army and was used to marching. But he laughed at me when I suggested that his military service had probably prepared him for the trails we were about to use.

"No way," he said. "The army had nothing like this."

On the trail that morning, Mick was in the lead position and Adrian was in the position called, without derogatory intent, "Number Two." I was told that I had one task only: to keep up.

Roy ran up the slope, but instead of pausing at the top, he kept on running, racing along the trail through narrow gaps in jauntily flowered bushes with grabby thorns, then dashing along a creek bed over slimy mossy rocks before sprinting up yet another muddy bank, while I grasped at branches and ferns to stay close. After running for what felt like a very long time, I wanted to ask how normal this pace was and how long it could be expected to last. Unfortunately, someone had let a swarm of scorpions loose in my lungs and I couldn't speak, so I just grimly sprinted on, wondering if it was considered rude to vomit.

By the end of the morning session, I noticed Mick and Adrian shooting surreptitious glances at each other. I wondered if their exchanges meant that this was worse than Roy's usual new-wrangler hazing, and if they figured they should see if I could tough it out. My lungs were still on fire, but I took comfort in the thought that it wouldn't get harder than this.

At lunchtime, Mick and I staggered back to the main area while Adrian waited with Roy, who had the run of an exercise area during our break. My body demanded protein after such abuse, but the meal was disappointingly vegetarian. We sat side by side, no one else apparently wanting to sit next to such conspicuously perspiring men.

I had come to Parque Machia out of a desire to do some good and have some fun at the same time, but doubt filled my mind as I gasped between bites. I was still sure that I could do something positive, but I wondered about my capacity to enjoy running with Roy. That afternoon I decided I'd simply endure my time with Roy and put it down as an experience I'd never have had if I'd stayed behind a desk in Sydney.

I slept a bone-weary sleep that night in the rudimentary accommodations offered at the park, my exhaustion overpowering a disturbing ache in my right knee. One of the symptoms of my being ill-suited for suburban life had been an aversion to refrigerator ownership. I had tolerated it, but I had never gotten over the feeling that a fridge was a shackle to a particular place. That night, however, I yearned for the ice that would normally be found in such an appliance. Why, at thirty-four, would I choose to put myself through this? Who the hell is afraid of a fridge but ties himself to a puma? I had been away from full-time safari work for almost a decade, and the break had let me revert to my natural state—weak-kneed, soft handed, and fearful. The work was noble. I loved the philosophy of Inti Wara Yassi: No animal deserved to live its life in a cage. But perhaps I had been a fool when I raised my hand for Roy. Then again, the worst decisions have usually led to my best adventures. I would care for that puma or disintegrate trying.

The next morning I got up at six and dragged myself down the short stretch of road to the cafe where the volunteers gathered each morning before starting their day. Most of them were far younger than I and bustled around with an energy I couldn't hope to muster at that hour of the morning without snorting instant coffee (something that should never be tried, even for a dare).

Some of the volunteers tended to monkeys that had been rehabilitated and released into the reserve but still needed some care and observation. Others tended to the capuchins, spider monkeys, and squirrel monkeys that had only recently arrived and still required time in quarantine.

Some of the volunteers sitting around the breakfast table shouted like artillerymen, deafened perhaps by the parrots in their care. Then there were those who worked in an area given the innocuous-sounding name of "small animals." These included coatis—a relative of the raccoon with a short prehensile snout—and a badger-size relative of the weasel called a tayra. While each of these species was capable of displaying great affection to its caretakers, both were equally as well-known for turning savage and using their sharp teeth to inflict grievous wounds.

By volunteering to spend time with Roy, I'd joined the last group at the table, the cat people, and my compatriots were openly envious of some of these wounds. While not keen on pain, a scar did seem a great souvenir of this experience. Yet I was told the cats, including Roy who was the wildest of the four pumas at Machia, rarely bit hard enough to draw blood.

Despite this assurance, within two days I was able to show off some marks on my left knee, and I'd still not taken the cord, or lead position. For reasons never apparent Roy liked to select just one knee on each of the volunteers who worked with him and stuck to assaulting that knee alone, regardless of which was closest. Roy fancied my left.

When at last I took the cord position with Roy, I tried not to show my nervousness while sweat that had nothing to do with heat poured from my torso and brow. Roy jumped me three times that first morning. Being tied to him naturally made me an easier target. No matter how many times I'd seen it happen to Mick and Adrian, there was nothing that could prepare me for the moment the puma stopped running, turned and faced me with pupils contracted, and launched lightning fast at my leg.

Pumas can bite much harder, and inflict much more pain, than Roy does, so I shouldn't have really been that disturbed. But a very primal part of me protested that what I was doing was silly and illogical and that the rope should just be cut. Some ancestral lizard inside me uncurled and squeaked to undo the rope, climb a tree, and stay away from anything large with fur and fangs. Let the puma run free! Or whatever it was he wanted to do in exchange for not biting me.

But Roy could not be set free because, like many of the animals at Parque Machia, and the other parks run by Inti Wara Yassi, he was too young when he arrived to ever be able to survive in the wild. His mother had most likely been killed for her skin at a time when Roy and his brother were far too young to fend for themselves. The strain of capture, confiscation, and relocation had proved too much for Roy's brother, and he died soon after arriving.

Roy, though, had thrived and was renowned among the organization's volunteers as the most demanding puma in the four parks managed by Inti. Demanding or not, he needed daily runs to maintain his health and to give him a better life than he would have had if he was locked in a cage day after day.

"You *have* to keep him on the rope at all costs," Mick had explained to me. "He got off once; nobody will ever say how. Roy's a racist, hates Bolivians, and when he escaped, the first person he saw was a local guy. He took his spleen out with a single swipe. If something like that ever happens again, the place will be shut down and all these animals will just get sold off to zoos by the local council."

Right, I thought determined to quash the impulse to release Roy, *keep him on the rope at all costs.*

Despite knowing that Roy had never had a trainer he hadn't jumped, I thought I might become one of the people he jumped less often—for two reasons. I'd had a cat in Australia named Tyson. Tyson had been my fiancée's, and he died soon after my relationship ended. Losing him was almost as big an emotional blow as the breakup; I loved him dearly and had studied his habits and personality with affectionate interest. I was sure my understanding of a house cat would be partly transferrable to a puma. Also, since I'd spent plenty of time with lions, leopards, and cheetahs—and wild ones, at that—I felt sure I wouldn't be scared of Roy. Roy would pick up on my lack of fear, and we'd become great friends, surprising the many previous volunteers who'd spent time with him and allowing me to share some of the awe that surrounded conversations about Roy. I missed Tyson and wanted that sort of relationship again. We'd be friends, Roy and me, just like Tyse and I had been, I was sure.

Sure.

2

Roy's Big Day Out

The strain of running nine to fifteen miles a day on difficult jungle terrain soon took a toll on my body. When Bondy had said Roy's handlers needed to be fit, I'd believed I was. Now I knew that was because I'd never been to a gym where the trainer bit you for running too slowly. Roy's handlers were perpetually soaked in sweat, a result of humidity so intense that breathing felt more like drowning. The closed-canopy rain forest under which we ran was quite beautiful, even if it was stifling. It rang with the chatter of monkeys and clatter of woodpeckers, while streams ran clear from the peaks we tackled as part of Roy's routine.

■ ■

"See that twitch?" said Mick, after I'd been there about a week.

"Yep," I replied. Roy's front right leg had a definite quiver in it after one of his rare moments of inactivity. But as predators are hardwired not to show weakness, he did his best to hide it, even putting full weight onto what was obviously a pained limb to slow the tremor.

"It's gonna need to be checked by one of the vets," said Mick.

Roy's annual veterinary checkup wasn't due for another month, but it had to be rescheduled for the following week so his leg could be examined properly.

An X-ray machine was as far out of Inti Wara Yassi's budget as a space shuttle, so Roy had to go to the hospital. Without any veterinary hospitals within reasonable distance, there was only one place for him to go: a human hospital more than twelve miles away.

Unfortunately, another piece of equipment Inti Wara Yassi lacks is a vehicle.

■ ■

"So, we're going in a taxi?" I asked, smiling, on the day of Roy's X-ray.

"*Si*," replied one of the few permanent staff, a hardworking vet named Luis.

"Does the driver know that not all his passengers are human?" I asked.

"*Si*," Luis said again, keeping to his pattern of not speaking English until the drinks started flowing. Then he would become perfectly fluent, a startling change.

So it was that Roy was anesthetized and painstakingly manhandled down near vertical drops and slippery-sloped trails on a stretcher. Along with two vets, plus Mick and Bondy (who'd decided it was too good a sight to miss), I clambered into the back of a station wagon taxi, its seats folded down to take the stretcher and its cargo. A small crowd, hoping to catch a glimpse of the famous Roy, drew around us as we set off, The only person seemingly not impressed by Roy was the taxi driver, who acted as if nothing was out of the ordinary and soon had us rumbling along the rutted road until we left the tar and hit an even more jangly stretch of cobblestone, flanked by dank jungle.

After a while we came to a roadblock where soldiers who looked like mere teens were wielding machine guns—a fine incentive for us to stop. I wasn't sure what they were after—drugs, bribes, some zit cream—but doubted we had the papers to prove we were legitimately able to transport a puma via taxi.

"Drug checkpoint," Bondy said flatly.

I looked at Luis, who held a loaded syringe low in his hand, a bead of moisture glistening at its tip. *Well, that doesn't look at all suspicious,* I thought. The soldiers approached with grim expressions, one holding something that looked a little like a corkscrew in his hand.

"They use that thing to stick into people's luggage and get a sample of what's inside," Mick explained.

As they drew closer, the soldiers had a good look at our pile of bodies, but not at Roy, whose only exposure was his tail tip, occasionally twitching as he dreamed of chasing knees through a field.

"Dare you to use it," Mick calmly challenged the soldiers with their sampling tool as they drew in, and he whipped back the blanket. Roy's eyes were frozen in the very same stare he used when about to attack, and both soldiers jumped back.

"Puma!" one of them exclaimed, quite unnecessarily.

In rapid-fire and urgent-sounding Spanish, Luis quickly explained our mission, but also that we had to hurry, as the puma could wake up at any moment and might become dangerous, showing the needle to emphasize his point.

They quickly waved us on, the look of mingled glee and excitement on their faces at seeing such an animal highlighting how young they were and how much of an aura even a sleeping puma possesses.

Finally arriving at the hospital, we rushed Roy through the swinging doors, mindful as ever of his tail, around a corner into a windowless corridor whose light fixtures had more blown bulbs than lit ones.

We were met by a man wearing a beanie. He had a pair of glasses perched on his nose with lenses of such remarkable thickness that his neck must have felt the strain of the weight of them.

"*Radioliga*," Luis explained, and even with my limited Spanish I could guess at his profession.

We carefully lifted Roy off the stretcher and laid him out across the radiologist's table. Roy's eyes were still wide, and on occasion he would rumble through rubbery lips. While I stood over the table, the radiologist backed away, and I wondered if he knew about Roy's legendary despleening. But then I heard a switch being flicked followed by an indistinct buzzing. Glancing over, I was appalled to see the radiologist behind a screen, presumably lead, and a nurse there too. Surely they should have warned us before releasing radioactive waves. But no, the radiologist spoke to the vets, who repositioned Roy, and again with no preamble he flicked the switch. I was sure I felt hair growing on parts of my body where it had never grown before.

"Bloody hell," Mick said. "I think my nuts just shrank!"

It was only then that I noticed the radiologist was missing an arm from the elbow down. I nudged Bondy, "Do you think he's met Roy before?"

We laughed; then the machine fired yet again, causing us to leave the room in a hurry, shooting spiteful glances at the one-armed man and covering our jewels as we went.

Once the plates were taken, the vets, who had stoically stayed in the room during the procedure, ushered us back in and we stretchered Roy out. News of his presence in the hospital had spread, and a small crowd had gathered once again. Visitors, nurses, children, and patients in sickly green robes clustered in the hall. It was easy to be angry with Bolivians in general for what they had done to all the animals that had ended up at the park, but these people showed a real awe at seeing Roy. I wondered if this had become an educational opportunity, a small step to raise awareness of the need for puma preservation. It was impossible to know, but I was glad to be there and waved as we all climbed into the back of the waiting taxi.

"Ciao!" a small child shouted cheerily, and soon the gathered crowd all started waving, saying ciao to the big cat they'd just met.

As the taxi began to pull away I waved and called, "Ciao!"

"Ciao!" echoed Bondy.

"Meow!" shouted Mick.

■ ■

Roy showed signs of waking on the ride back and was given another sedative. Though no doubt traumatic for him, the drive was just as stressful for those of us wedged into a confined space with an unpredictable puma.

With slightly jangled nerves we arrived at the drug checkpoint again. There were more soldiers than before, and we were waved away from the other cars into a sinister-looking section of the checkpoint out of sight of the road. A soldier with more stripes than the others then approached.

Bugger, I thought, *we're in trouble.* Paperwork could take hours in a place like this, hours and perhaps bribes that none of us had. I wasn't sure how long we could keep Roy under, either, or if Luis had planned for a long delay.

The officer pulled back the blanket that covered Roy, gave a hmmph of triumph, then turned to his assembled men and said something. One of the soldiers whipped a small camera out of his pocket, and the officer quickly struck a pose beside Roy's form, had his portrait taken, said, "Gracias," and signaled us on.

I was to learn later that the region of Bolivia where Parque Machia is located is, after Ecuador and Peru, the third-largest coca-growing area in the world. The drug checkpoint we'd encountered on the way to and from the hospital was a permanent fixture, a necessity in order for Bolivia to continue receiving U.S. aid. However, since it was known to everyone in the area and beyond, it was about as effective as a fish-scented deodorant.

Unfortunately, the local coca growers, supported by the mayor, had started to build a road around the checkpoint, bulldozing a swathe through the jungle, at one point even toppling trees onto an enclosure where monkeys were being rehabilitated. If completed, the road had the potential to shut down Parque Machia altogether, resulting in some animals having to be moved to other reserves run by Inti Wara Yassi.

By law in the event that animals needed to be moved, the mayor would be in a position to dictate which animals left and which stayed. The tourists who came to the area often expressed dismay that they were not allowed near the pumas or ocelots. Undoubtedly the mayor would want to keep some, and they would need to be kept in cages, because without volunteers there would be no one to walk the animals every day.

And only the rainy season was holding back the completion of the coca-growers road.

■ ■

The results of the X-ray revealed that Roy was suffering from a serious calcium deficiency, most likely congenital. "Man, his bones looked like a bird's," said Rob, a Californian who spent several months of each year donating his time to Inti Wara Yassi and had known Roy for years. He had no formal veterinary degree but had become somewhat of an expert on captive big cats. Rob and the vets devised a plan to supplement Roy's daily diet of chicken and beef with calcium powder. To prevent him from avoiding his medicine, the calcium powder had to be smeared all over Roy's food each day, a revolting job for me, Adrian, Mick, and any future Roy Boys (as we were collectively known).

"I'm not sure I want him getting any stronger," I said to Adrian as we trudged up the trail to Roy's cage one morning, a challenging path in itself that still left me panting, despite the fitness I was gaining daily.

"Me neither, but you know something?" said Adrian. "Now that I know Roy isn't well I feel a bit differently toward him. I'm not so angry with him when he's being a bastard."

I was surprised by Adrian's turn of sentiment, and wished I felt the same way. But contrary to my hopes, it had become apparent that I was a target for Roy's aggression. My knowledge of house cats was worse than useless and my lack of fear was not in the least bit charming. Roy was known to jump some people more than others—and I was one of those people. I held no dislike for Roy, but no affection either. I just wanted to make it through each day, getting jumped as little as possible.

Initially I'd considered staying longer than four weeks at Parque Machia, maybe even settling in this patch of Bolivian jungle for a few months. But after dealing with Roy for a while, I just wanted to get through the time I'd signed on for to prove to myself that a cat couldn't beat me.

3

Don't Eat My Hero

Roy's calcium regimen was well established when everyone at Parque Machia entered a state of nervous anticipation, the entire place humming with activity. We were expecting a visitor, one known to anyone with more than a passing interest in wildlife. Jane Goodall, whose famed research into chimpanzees had changed the way we think about apes, ourselves, and how wildlife research was conducted, was visiting for a night. Accompanying her would be Juan Carlos, the founder of Inti Wara Yassi. Juan Carlos's benevolence had also extended to runaways and orphaned children, and some of these children would be there to meet Jane as well.

While others did their best to buff and polish cages, counters, and containment areas—all of which the monkeys immediately befouled—Mick and I took Roy out for his morning round. Mick was leaving the park in the next few days and wanted as much time with Roy as possible, to the delight of Adrian who'd been given a day off the trail that he could spend lazing at the tourist aviary, a dull job but one that involved no hills or bites—unless you were outwitted by a macaw.

I was in lead position, which meant the rope went directly from Roy's collar to my waist, with sturdy carabineers holding it in place at both ends. Though the rope was thirty-three feet, it was never willingly fed out to full length, and my aim was to keep it coiled in my left hand with little more than three feet granted to Roy for most of the walk, more when we went down steep hills and much less as we approached his "hot zones," what we called his regular, inexplicable places of attack. Mick stayed as close to my heels as he could without tripping me, close enough that if Roy did jump me, he would be there right away to lead him off once I had dislodged his paws.

The walk started well, and I thought that after two weeks maybe Roy was getting used to me and perhaps I was getting better at judging his moods and reading his body language, anticipating his jumps and blocking his turns. My knee was still regularly abused, but not as often as at the start of my tenure. So it was with confidence that I tackled one of the toughest parts of the trail, which involved dropping my full body length onto a narrow ledge, then immediately leaping onto a well-polished log that traversed a sheer rock face, using the momentum to jump again onto moderately firmer ground. This was followed directly by a run and jump onto a rock, with a well-timed grab at a tree to keep from sliding down a ledge. Three paces later came a tight squeeze between two vertical rock faces, made worse by the slippery surface underfoot where water pooled. This was one of the first times I'd remembered to get close to Roy right after the gap, which was important, as he always attempted a left turn at that point, even though the trail went right.

"Pete? Mick?" came a voice ahead of us.

Roy froze, his ears pivoting forward and locking in the voice's direction.

"Yep?" Mick shouted back.

The voice belonged to Bec, who worked with a puma named Sonko. Sonko was fat, and the Roy Boys delighted in pointing out his bulk, thereby not so subtly indicating that Roy was the *real* puma.

"Sonko is lying down, hasn't moved for half an hour!" Bec shouted to us.

"Kick him!" Mick shouted back.

Sonko's volunteers treated Mick's suggestion with the seriousness it deserved, and so we found ourselves at an impasse. The two pumas' trails overlapped in many places, and these spots nearly flowed with the territorial markings of two alpha males trying to outdo each other. Pumas are solitary by nature, and two male pumas never get together casually to discuss sports or girls. They only come together to fight over land. If Roy and Sonko were to meet, it would be catastrophic, so we needed to do something—and fast.

Roy, Mick, and I stood at the top of a steep gully, the base of which was covered with smooth river rocks. The other riverbank was more vegetated, but not too far up it linked with our trail again. If we cut down the bank then scrambled up the other side, somehow coaxing Roy ahead of us, we would overtake Sonko without his ever laying eyes on Roy.

I turned Roy back in the very direction I'd just denied him, and his pace immediately picked up. Every day he aimed for this route, and every day he was refused. As we reached the riverbank, he moved even faster, and my boots scrabbled for purchase on the moss-covered rocks. Roy's four points on the ground made him far more sure-footed than I was, not to mention that he had evolved for such terrain and I have a noted lack of coordination.

"Try to steer him up the bank here," called Mick. But the rope had run out, and swinging my arm to the right barely influenced Roy's path.

Roy continued on faster still, and with no way of slowing him down without stopping, I was forced to let more rope play out, even though more than half had already slid roughly through my palm. At this point the riverbed was level, but ahead was a downward slope and a trail used by some of Inti's other animals. Over the sounds of jungle insects and the ever-present, strangely electronic burbling of a bird called an orependola, came a sound I hadn't imagined hearing here. It was children somewhere out of sight singing to Jane Goodall.

Suddenly I was struck by a horrifying vision of Roy attacking my childhood hero or one of the poor little orphans that fate had already mistreated. I upped my pace considerably, with Mick still right behind me even though the going was just as tough for him.

But Roy was faster than the both of us and hit the slope at a sprint, his intent ominous. The rope pulled tight, and despite Roy's weight being less than mine, I was pulled clean off my feet, landing facedown and headfirst before starting a sideways drag that was injurious to both pride and skin. By this point Roy was already over the hill's crest, and as I reached it I clutched at a wrist-thick tree, gripping with all the strength of my left hand and yanking us to a halt.

I looked down at Roy, who glanced back, his face set in the exact visage he wore whenever he was about to cause mayhem. He jerked his body sideways with such incredible strength that the tree, still in my grip, tore from the ground—and then Roy started dragging me along again. The sensation was like being dumped by a wave, but without the cushioning softness of water. I smashed against rocks, bounced over stumps, and got friction burn from the dirt and sharp grass tussocks. My whole body was so battered that I had no idea which part of it suddenly connected with a rock and somehow, mercifully, bounced me upright for a brief moment.

I took a running step but immediately lost my balance again, the rope at my waist yanking me at an odd angle. To my right was a tree, this one far larger than the one I'd grabbed previously, probably about the thickness of a telephone pole. Grabbing it one-handed was out of the question, so with the last bit of power available to me, I launched at it bodily, hoping to plaster myself like a skydiving koala against its rough bark. As with many of my athletic endeavors, I sailed wide of the mark. This left the rope bent around the trunk in a U, with Roy's momentum on one side and mine on the other. For once my weight mattered, and Roy's advance was brought to a halt as the rope pulled tight—and I was slammed against the tree. I fell prone, using the tree and my heft as a brake, and watched Mick run past, to calm and collect Roy.

Before I could decide not to, I stood up. Wincing and spitting dirt from my teeth, I joined Mick and the still wide-eyed Roy.

"You can walk?" Mick asked, genuinely incredulous.

"Since I was about a year old, actually," I replied, most likely in shock.

"I was sure you must have broken something," said Mick.

"Not sure that I haven't," I replied.

In fact I thought it might just be adrenaline holding me upright, but I wanted to get Roy away from the orphans before I checked.

It turned out that my misadventure had resulted in only bruises, abrasions, and welts, and I was well enough to attend the dinner in honor of Jane that evening. I was now wearing a shirt so Jane didn't have to see my injuries, but she seemed grateful when I told her, in as offhanded a way as I could manage, about the day's events.

Right there and then, talking to Jane, a woman who still travels three hundred days of the year to promote conservation even though she's now in her seventies, I decided that complaining about bumps and bruises was fine, but it was time to stop worrying about my age. Sure, aging was a bastard, but as long as my knees held out and my lungs drew air, I would make sure to enjoy every moment I was beaten up by a half-wild puma, because it was so much better than being beaten down by a desk.

4

Dressed for a Kill

The next day was Mick's last with Roy, and he took the cord for the whole day. I filmed much of it, in the hope he would have a memento of one of Roy's jumps besides the scarring on his mangled right knee. But Roy behaved like a kitten, never even attempting an attack, just trotting politely along the trails, responding with affection whenever Mick drew close. (Roy, like all cats, showed he liked you by bumping his head against yours—this isn't fun if it's an English soccer fan, and it's only marginally more so when it's a puma.)

At the end of the afternoon walk, Mick said good-bye to Roy, ending his heroically long six-week stint with him. Mick's eyes were watery as he walked away, but I didn't even feel like mocking him. In truth I was perplexed by his apparent love for this ill-tempered animal.

I had loved many animals in the past, more than I could count, but however much the times when I came close to an elephant or a lion had meant to me, close contact had always been exceptional. Mostly I could love animals, apart from pets, from a distance. I knew that the animals I'd observed daily in Botswana might kill me if I approached them, but I never felt any malice from them; the distance meant that such an attack would never be personal.

Roy was different—neither a pet, nor exactly wild. I couldn't shake the feeling that his abuse was deliberate, vindictive even. A lion charge might kill me, but I'd never suffered them every day. Roy was probably not going to kill me, but he was hurting me several times a week.

Mick's departure made it worse. Adrian and I kept running with Roy, hoping a suitable candidate to help us out would soon appear. Meanwhile, with no one to give us a rest, we had to slog through day after day. And Roy seemed to have fallen into a foul mood. He was jumping us at every hot zone, and quite often in areas outside them as well.

Each morning Adrian and I would sit at breakfast, shooting shifty glances at the clock that was moving too fast to the hour when we would have to face the walk to Roy's cage.

One day Roy bit me a record four times—and made another six attempts I was able to block—making me seriously wonder why I'd ever signed up for such an ordeal. The notion of doing good seemed like faint reward.

■ ■

"This place sucks," said Jodie, an American girl who worked in the monkey quarantine area, across the lunch table one day. "They have too many animals, and hardly any get released. It sucks," she said again, taking an aggressive drag of her cigarette.

Though she was giving voice to my very own feelings, as soon as I heard them, I felt the need to argue.

"It does if you think that the sole aim is to release animals," I replied. "But most injured wild animals die. And most of the ones brought here to Inti have injuries too severe to ever be released again, or they have no habitat to return to. If they're not going to be locked in a cage or euthanized, giving them the best possible life they can have is the only option."

Jodie nodded at me, reluctantly agreeing, and I continued on enthusiastically. What she'd said had prompted the surfacing of some ideas I'd been muddling over that might give some purpose to what we were doing.

"If at the end of the day you can believe that one animal's life is better, even if just for that day, because of what you have done, then why not be happy with that?" I added. We both knew that Inti would never refuse an animal care and that we were doing what we could for every one of them.

She nodded again, and so did I, having convinced myself as much as her. Roy wasn't to blame for the way he behaved. Inti couldn't afford trainers and aimed merely for Roy, the monkeys, Baloo the bear, the birds, and the nasty small animals to be as wild as they could be given they couldn't be wild. Their mission was flawed, but noble.

Bloody hell, I thought, so was Roy.

Responding to Jodie's challenge made me feel renewed somewhat, and that afternoon I approached Roy with a different mindset. It wasn't his fault that his mother had been killed, and I couldn't blame him for wanting to be wild and puma-like. I should embrace it, embrace it all—the charges, the bites, the rolling around to gain more rope so he could jump me, and the awkward moments when he stared into my eyes while defecating.

I'd often said I liked animals so much because they would never hurt you out of malice—that they don't recognize that we *feel,* so they can't intentionally inflict pain or fear. Roy's behavior often felt malicious to me, but I knew better, knew enough not to anthropomorphize him, knew enough to appreciate him as a puma. I just had to try to remember that each time he latched on to my leg.

The walk that afternoon went well, with only a few jump attempts, all pretty halfhearted at best. It was most likely coincidence, but I felt like Roy and I had made a breakthrough, and things seemed to be looking up even more when Adrian and I were granted a trainee. When we got the trainee ready—which would take at least four days—we could start having the occasional day for our legs to recover. My mood was heading toward buoyant. With a day's break I might just make it through the remaining two weeks of my stay.

That night there was a party, and I let myself go more than a little with a nasty local brew called Singani, made primarily of cane sugar and Satan's urine (at least that was the theory I developed in my throbbing head the next day). I hoped it was just my alcohol-addled ears deceiving me when I heard what sounded like an auction. Next thing I knew the item being bid on was me.

"Wha . . . ?" I asked eloquently.

Bondy, who was acting as auctioneer, explained. The Roy Boys were for sale. Being sufficiently stupid or macho to volunteer to run with Roy made us the perfect victims. The money raised would be put toward the animals.

I mumbled something about my discomfort at being sold as a slave when I already suffered daily indignities at the paws of Roy and the trail itself, but this fell on deaf ears.

The bids climbed, admittedly at a sloth's pace, and I watched as a Swiss girl of volatile temperament took the lead. I was quite nervous that she might not comprehend there were some things I wouldn't do, even for charity.

To my enormous relief a coalition formed in challenge to her bid, and I was ultimately sold to a group of four women who immediately set about devising their plan for the twenty-four-hour period I would belong to them.

Adrian was also sold, and I watched his face deflate like a balloon when the Swiss girl made the winning bid.

"Bad luck, mate," I consoled. "Can't imagine the demands I get will be as bad as yours."

First up for me as a slave was cooking dinner, something I thought might well be more hazardous for my purchasers than for me. Massages were also ordered and performed. But then came the clincher: I was required, just for my owners' amusement, to wear a dress. And not just any dress. Despite the small size of the town near the reserve, it had a store that sold secondhand clothes and costumes. From its stock a pink checkerboard schoolgirl's dress had been selected. It was lurid and tight in the most uncomfortable places.

"I think we need to talk about rugby a lot today," I said as I emerged in my gorgeous new ensemble to the jeers and hoots of all the volunteers. To make an attack on the machismo of the Roy Boys had been part of the auction's design, and my owners were following through with the logic. "I may need to overcompensate for this to find out if I have any testosterone left." However macho Roy Boys are, I had never felt myself to be much of an example of the breed in this respect. As I plucked at the stifling Lycra underwear sewn into the skirt, I started to explain some of Roy's quirks to John, our new trainee.

"You know," John interrupted, "I can't really take in any of what you're saying seriously while you're wearing that."

"Right," I said. "Adrian, maybe you better go over it all. I'll just machete some vines or something."

Roy, of course, paid no attention to my apparel. Like most animals he wasn't interested in clothing unless it smelled peculiar. Maybe he felt some smug satisfaction at seeing me in it. ("Who's got the feminine features *now?*" I could imagine him asking.) He greeted us the same way he did every morning, eyeing John with a look I'd seen before, the same look lions give baby impalas and Roy had given me when I began.

"Let's see what sort of mood he's in," I said as we approached the first hill in Roy's walking area. "Keep up if you can, John," I said, just as Roy bolted.

By now Adrian and I were used to the footholds, knew which trees to grab and which not to, including the "Bastard Tree," which was covered in vicious spines concealed under beards of lichen. You only grabbed this tree once. John didn't know the trees or the trail, and I heard his curses and then a solid *THWAP* as he slipped.

"Not good," Adrian said simply.

Roy barely paused as we entered into one of his hot zones—places where the terrain required us to let out some more rope, giving him a better chance to turn and bite us—at which point I grew nervous that he was just getting his energy levels back up for some serious jumping.

He was. I wasn't on lead, so Adrian took the brunt of it. But as the number two guy, my job was to be there to make sure I got Roy off of him fast. The moment I had him off Adrian, he jumped me. Adrian pulled him off, and Roy went straight for Adrian again.

We finally got him through the zone and had a few minutes' respite, jogging but not sprinting.

Once he had the breath to speak, Adrian added to his earlier verdict: "Not good at all."

I grunted my agreement and trotted along behind him, offering words of encouragement to John, who was struggling to keep up with us by now.

"Frankly I think it's lunatic to go out every day into the jungle when there's a very good chance that a puma will bite you," John said at the end of the walk. "I think you're both mad."

"I don't suppose I can argue with that while wearing this," I said, plucking at the dress again with one hand and reaching for the machete with the other, in the hope of looking more butch.

"You look like Braveheart's gay cousin," John commented.

I was worried that John might quit and leave us without a substitute. Two days later he did, limping off with a sprained ankle, so that once again it was just Adrian and me, plagued by fatigue and footrot, and Roy, unfazed by anything except when we managed to block his attempts in the hot zones.

Soon afterward we had a scorchingly hot day (the dress was fortunately relegated to the trash can as soon as my day of humiliation was over), the sort that raised beads of sweat on your brow just at the thought of action. Despite the fact that our perspiration would stream down our bodies and fill our boots, Adrian and I liked these days. In these conditions the trail was exhausting enough for us, but Roy had to do it wearing a fur coat, and this helped us predict his behavior. He usually ran little on very hot days, and, most lovely of all, jumped us a lot less often.

But, as usual, Roy defied our expectations that day and took off at a punishing pace. Eventually we crossed a particularly slippery part of trail before dropping down to a creek bed with a series of small falls and crystal-clear pools. Ferns acted as parasols overhead, and the jungle rang with cries of alarm from the monkeys.

The heat had finally taken its toll on him, and Roy immersed himself in one of the pools, so I gently scooped some water into my hands and trickled it over his head and ears until he flicked his tail, letting me know he'd had enough.

Suddenly from down the creek came the strange sound of a small motor and a flash of green and purple, zigging beelike before zagging away, almost too fast to glimpse, certainly too quick to scrutinize. It was a hummingbird, and, to my utter delight, it hovered within inches of Roy's head, directly over his open countenance. It held itself there before scooting over to Adrian, where it paused briefly in front of his face, before repeating the performance with me, fanning my face with manic wing beats. Then with a whir of wings and a pop of color, it was gone. It was such a rare moment, something so hard to explain, so beautiful and wonderful and unexpected. A jewel in time.

"Wow," I said, to Roy, to Adrian, to myself.

"Nice," said Adrian.

Roy didn't react at all to the bird. Instead he just stood up, shook himself off like a dog, spraying Adrian and me in the process, and set off again, refreshed enough that he even made a half-hearted jump along the trail. But my mood couldn't be dampened, and I felt a flicker of enjoyment.

"Good boy," I said to Roy, and to my surprise, I meant it.

5

The Last Temptation of Roy

Over the next few days, something strange happened. Roy's hot zones went cold. At the approach to each hot zone, an anticipatory noise like the zinging of violins would start in my ears, but Roy now just strolled through, not even glancing back at us to see if we were lagging behind enough for him to wreak havoc.

Each day when either Adrian or I went to get food for lunch, someone would ask us how Roy was behaving. For two and a half days we had to disappoint by reporting, "He's turned into a Labrador. Did nothing. Just walked the trails."

I started patting him whenever I had the chance, and even bumped heads with him on occasion, happy that he returned the affection. It was as if I had passed a test, and now we had a bond impossible to imagine a few weeks previous. Whether all the early jumping had been to assert dominance, or to try to drive me away, I didn't know. Regardless, I was glad for the reprieve and used the word *bastard* a lot less often when talking about Roy to the other volunteers.

But then my backside changed everything.

There was a particular section of trail I'd long dreaded—for two reasons. One was that it provided Roy with the choice of extending the punishment of our daily routine by several miles. The other was that it had a drop that required great timing and balance to negotiate, two things sadly missing from my genetic makeup. To handle the drop, I had to make sure I was right behind Roy, because he tended to sprint as soon as he hit the ground. If the rope pulled tight while I was in midair I was likely to be pasted onto a tree. Failing that, I would often launch off the drop weak-limbed, land floppily, and miss the handhold tree that was a few feet or so down the path.

What typically followed was some cartwheeling of legs, and an inelegant flailing for handholds, but on this day my feet shot forward and I landed heavily on my derriere. The ground was muddy and slippery, and I soon began an uncontrollable slide down the trail. Roy had settled into a fast walk when he saw movement beside him. It was me, sliding right past him. This was something way too tempting for any puma to ignore.

"Hi Roy!" I said in as even a tone as you can when your shorts are torn open, mud is filling your underpants, and a puma is eyeing you like you're so mad the only sensible response is to bite you. And bite me he did.

Roy's teeth on my leg stopped my slide, but this time he hit me a little higher than usual and got me in the thigh. I now knew how much more painful a tooth into muscle is than a tooth into bone. I shouted out something that is considered rude in most languages and shoved at Roy's head.

Adrian rushed up and grabbed the free portion of the lead, which allowed me to lift my knee and remove Roy's paws so I could try to hobble after him instead of getting tipped again. As he did so often after a jump, Roy sprinted, and only then did I see that there were barely three feet of free cord between Roy and me; the rest was somehow coiled around Roy's body. The rope pulled tight, but I was already running. Roy turned, frustrated at my slow pace, and jumped at me again. This time he hit me low and sent us both into a spin during which one of his claws dragged down my calf, taking my boot off with it.

Adrian appeared again in record time and grabbed at Roy's cord, freeing a loop that had formed around his body. The other loops pulled tight, and I found myself being dragged by a half-crazed puma once again. This time I nabbed his collar in time.

My pants were now shredded, the seat was flapping, and the section below the left knee was hanging by threads. It was one of the few occasions when Roy had drawn blood, and I could see a small bloom of red through some remaining fabric.

"Roy didn't like me falling over. He seems to have blamed my leg," I said, as thunder rumbled overhead.

A breeze kicked up, and Adrian and I both checked the sky through the canopy while keeping pace with our perturbed puma. An ominous swirling of foliage made it impossible to ignore that a drenching rain was on its way. The heaviest rains of the year were due soon, and this looked like it was going to be a potent warm-up act. Roy's fur stood on end as if he was electrified, and with the next clap of thunder he glanced our way, looking like we were to blame for the noise—or my knee was.

As the first fat splats of rain hit the canopy above, it became obvious that as far as Roy was concerned, the rain *was* my knee's fault. After nearly three days of peace and quiet, Roy jumped me three times in half an hour. My skin was starting to give way in uncomfortable directions. The weird thing was that I was actually starting to like him. The break from violence had allowed me to feel closer to him, and somehow the return of abuse didn't change that. Since I'd stopped focusing on my pain, and stopped blaming Roy for it, I could see that Roy jumped people because he was merely excitable. He loved these walks and had no other way of expressing himself other than by being a puma. However out of place I had felt behind a desk, he was more trapped between worlds than I had ever been and could not be blamed for behaving wildly.

The rain dissipated within a day, leaving as its legacy slippery-slope trails that even Roy took slowly, although he sped up well before we were ready to. Adrian and I were now exhausted, battered, and plagued with the strange rashes that come from constantly being wet. Our feet emerged from their boots each day prune-like, ghastly white, and sore to the touch. We were both near the end of our month and keen to move on to somewhere else. Physically I felt that any more time at Parque Machia would break me.

By a happy twist of fate, within two days two new potential trainees arrived and, following a trend, they were both Australians.

"So do you guys pat him?" the one named Courtney asked.

"Not so much," Adrian answered.

"Hmmph," said Courtney. And I knew that just like I had a month earlier, he was imagining that by the end of his stint he would have Roy wrapped around his little finger. The truth is that I did pat Roy, but not often, and only when we were in the safest areas. It was always a thrill for me, but a pat could excite him, and excitement would turn to a jump and a bite.

"Just so you know," I explained, "if you think you know how to handle a puma because you've owned a cat, you don't." I said, remembering my own earlier naiveté. "It would be like playing with sharks because you once owned a goldfish."

It only took Courtney one time on lead to shake his attitude. Roy's crazy face was unsettling enough, but just like me, Courtney wasn't prepared for the shock of actually being bitten by a puma. And Roy went after him, jumping him often and with a degree of venom I didn't recall experiencing from my own training, only a month before.

"You know what?" said Courtney after a few days. "I'm not interested in being his buddy anymore. I just want to make it through the month."

I grinned broadly back at him.

■ ■

When I left Machia, the rains came down like the day that everything had been my knee's fault. I was glad to get out before the rains hit too hard, glad to have time for my legs to recover from running so much, but I was wistful that I'd only just begun having fun with Roy and, I admit, started to like him as well. He was a real puma.

No longer vulnerable to his attacks, all I could think of was how vulnerable Roy was. I had no idea how much time Parque Machia would remain running before the desire for cocaine in far parts of the world shut it down. And I worried about whether the supply of Roy Boys, never abundant to begin with, would carry on the work. Strange as it might have seemed to me only a week before, on the day I left it wasn't just raindrops wetting my cheeks.

6

Not the End of the World

"Do you think Argentina is more like Switzerland or Ethiopia?" Freddy asked. My sister Laurie was visiting me in Argentina from Australia, and her friend Freddy and his wife had invited us to dinner.

I thought of the famous story of the Argentinian football players stranded after a plane crash who resorted to cannibalism in the bitter cold. I thought of condors soaring over the high Andes. I thought of fine Argentinean wine and the slopes where the grapes grew.

Switzerland seemed obvious, but Freddy seemed like the sort of person who enjoyed trick questions, so I answered Ethiopia.

"Exactly!" was Freddy's delighted reply. "Most of Argentina is desert—dry, horrible desert, barely worth farming. Only in the east and right at the south, in Patagonia, do you have mountains and snow."

Then and there I started to think of Patagonia as my next destination. I'd been staying with my friends Marguerite and Harris in Santiago, Chile, and the scars on my knee had faded. It looked like I'd been attacked by nothing more savage than acne. It was time for a new adventure.

In travelers' circles, and in some literary ones as well, Patagonia is famous for its stark landscapes, bleak winds, peaks capped with snow year-round, and the largest sheet of ice outside of the polar regions. Few animals survive there, but I thought I might be able to find pumas, penguins, seals, and orcas. It is meant to inspire soul-searching, even for someone like me who doesn't believe in a soul. Patagonia has a reputation as a destination of choice. Charles Darwin visited the island of Tierra del Fuego in the early 1800s and reported seeing no buildings, just the fires after which the island was named. He said the people were barely human, the most primitive he had ever seen. While I thought his comments about the people were racist (as if anything but high evolution would enable survival in such a place), I hoped that it signified a wildness I'd still be able to feel.

Laurie headed back to Australia, and I headed south to the Chilean town of Puerto Montt to take a flight to the farthermost reaches of Patagonia. I'd settled on the town of Ushuaia, the world's southernmost city, as my first destination. I might see condors up close there.

My entrance into Ushuaia, which involved flying through a cleft in jagged, white-capped mountains, made me feel uncharacteristically optimistic. Africa was never like this, and as an Australian I am easily impressed by mountains. These loomed with an impressive degree of beautiful menace, the sort of beauty a shark has, wild and untouchable. They were not just untrammeled, but untrammelable, which I realize is not a real word—but it is a very real feeling.

A sign in the airport that read, THE STORE AT THE END OF THE WORLD AT THE AIRPORT AT THE END OF THE WORLD, was a bad omen.

By the time I got to San Martin, the main drag of Ushuaia, I was wondering if Charles Darwin would have been even harsher with his criticism if he'd visited today. At least the locals hadn't tried to sell him anything. Hawkers squawked from the front of every bar and restaurant. Dinner deals! Happy hour specials! There was a whiff of desperation in some of the stores, which flogged Argentinean soccer jerseys, mate (the local tea) and its associated tea-making paraphernalia, addictive local red wine, and miniature dolls from cultures either gone or waning. I saw a group of cruise passengers rolling down the street like a human tsunami dressed in yellow and red windproof parkas, and realized that they would only stay a few hours—and then be replaced in a day or two in an ever-renewing group of tourists like wallets with legs.

I got a bed in a backpackers' hostel, where I was the most wizened creature, I imagined, that had stayed there in months. One evening I was talking to a young German named Friederike in the common room, expressing my dissatisfaction with Ushuaia.

"Maybe you've traveled too much. Perhaps you are too hard to impress now. I worry the same will happen to me," she said.

Maybe I was just too old for this near-hobo existence. Jane Goodall might be spry in her seventies, but at my age she'd already accomplished things I never had.

Perhaps a scientist could help me stifle such misgivings. Freddy's wife had a zoologist niece named Marcella who was studying the breeding habits of Chilean swallows. I had taken some day trips from Ushuaia to seek the isolation I'd sought in Patagonia and had been left feeling dissatisfied. The place was simply too developed for my liking and seemed too fixated on its status when it in fact sat at a latitude no more extreme than Moscow or Glasgow. Marcella had been there a while, and she didn't mind me squelching along behind her through bogs as she checked the nests of Chilean swallows. This was as far south as any species of swallow went, so for them at least, this really was the end of the world, and Marcella's research probed that distinction.

I'd learned Ushuaia had a population of roughly twenty thousand people, not all of whom could possibly be in the trinket business, even if it felt that way, and I asked Marcella about the main source of employment.

"Hotel construction," Marcella replied, expertly plucking a newly hatched Chilean swallow from its nesting box, then blowing into her hands to keep it warm before dropping it into a small plastic bag, weighing it, marking a toe with nail polish, and returning it to its feathered and soft birthplace before repeating the process with a nest mate.

She paused as we tramped through the bog. Mud splashed high against her rubber boots and straight over the low tops of mine and into my socks. "And shops for the tourists," she added after she was done with the next batch of chicks.

"But the tourists come on boats and usually stay on board. What do they need hotels for?" I asked, spattering my leg in a vain attempt to shake mud from my shoe.

There was a pause as Marcella inspected another nest.

"Southern house wren," she replied, and I thought she was being quite cryptic until I realized she was waiting for me to jot that down on a sheet next to the corresponding nest box number.

Ushuaia's best gift was a number of bird species I'd never seen before, the wonderfully named flightless steamer duck among them, almost making up for a dearth of condors.

"The hotels are for the tourists the council hopes will come," Marcella carried on. "They need jobs for all the people now that the television factory has shut down."

To my amazement a television factory had supported Ushuaia from the 1960s to the late 1990s. I imagined the industry as a cover for the sort of villain who appears in James Bond films. One of the nearby mountains could conceal the villain's underground lairs. Then again, those villains liked their comforts. This place was just too cold.

And this was midsummer. Snow topped the mountains still, and no sensible person would contemplate going outside without many layers of clothes. Even when the temperature rose above freezing, the ceaseless wind negated that gift.

■ ■

The flight out of Ushuaia was as beautiful and exciting as the one in, mountains clutching at the plane's wingtips as it climbed, climbed, climbed above the snow, before dipping almost immediately into an area called El Calafate. I'd wanted something more from Ushuaia, the feeling of isolation that Patagonia was famed for, a feeling of wildness, but hadn't been able to find it. The civilization had just been too pronounced, and that was the very thing I was trying to escape.

7

The Empanada Disaster

Riding the bus into El Calafate, another Patagonian destination, I felt a tingle of excitement as I took in the surrounding landscape, which was bare but not in that manufactured, blasted way humans so often create. Instead it was bare in a way that suggested no machine could modify it. After the streets of Ushuaia, with all those trinkets that were as authentic and tacky as a porn star's moans, this felt special. It felt wild.

I suddenly saw a golden red, long-necked animal, which I recognized as a guanaco, the wild relative of the llama. Turning to my fellow passengers to see if anyone else was delighted, I saw nothing but bland impassivity. So a few minutes later when I spotted a rheas, a large flightless bird that was also new to me, I kept my face pressed to the glass and enjoyed the sight by myself, not losing my grin even when we hit a bump in the road and my head bounced against the window.

The landscape changed several times on our way into town, each change thrilling in how it was so different from the previous view—the plain yielding to clefted red rocks, then to rounded hills, then to views of distant forested mountains.

The main part of El Calafate turned out to be touristy, with buildings made of rough-hewn timber that was triple varnished so it gleamed like no wood should. Still, I ventured down a side street to find the places where the locals ate, identifiable as such because they were crowded and no one was wearing branded outdoor gear.

As I ventured into an empanada store, the customers all went quiet, like the moment in a Western before a gunfight begins. Baleful stares and unhelpful waiters revealed I wasn't particularly welcome, but the food would be worth it. If you cater to locals, your food needs to be good—and cheap.

The store sold only empanadas. No pizzas, no burgers, no appeal-to-the-tourists llama steaks, just empanadas. If you wanted a soft drink, you had to cross the road to the general store.

I ordered six of the little pasties and ate them as I made my way to a lagoon I'd seen on a map of the region, cutting cross-country instead of taking the regular paved route.

It was a mistake, but an enlightening one.

Dust puffed from my heels as I walked, swirling up and away on the violent wind that caught the plastic bags that were omnipresent and pinned them to the bushes and trees. Empty bottles rolled by, glass ones tinkling, plastic ones drumming, while turkey vultures overhead simultaneously battled the gale and tried to determine what was dead and what was garbage. The neat street I had just come from seemed like deliberate fakery, like a pristine apple that is rotten under the skin.

The lagoon itself was beautiful but messy. Scattered among the ducks, coots, flamingos, and geese were pink, blue, and green shopping bags. I saw birds in the lagoon I had never seen before, but I worried for them, feeding amid such a lethal buffet.

As I walked around the lagoon's far side, I felt my stomach flop, then flip, then twist, then gurgle and splutter and ache. I had to clutch it because of the pain, all the while trying to focus on whether it really was a Chiloe wigeon I was looking at.

"It'll pass," I thought as my hands started to shake. I carried on watching the birds, saying hello to some horses, patting stray dogs that followed me everywhere. My lifelong affection for dogs—the first animals that I'd ever loved—helped me (mostly) to ignore their stink. Finally I headed back to the hostel, battling against the wind through litter-laden streets.

Sinister gurgles were emanating from my midsection by the time I reached the hostel. I thought if I lay down for a while they might pass.

They did not but rather remained with me through a dinner that I forced myself to eat because I figured I'd need the strength. I had a pricey ticket for the next day to hike on the Perito Moreno glacier.

I was in a shared room and had been allocated a top bunk over a sizable Italian woman with the most extraordinary frizzy gray hair. I felt sorry for her having to put up with my tossing and turning to try to find a position that was less painful. For the first time in years I felt genuinely lonely and homesick, but not for any place that I could name.

At two in the morning I felt as if I were being jabbed by spears, and I approached the front desk where, against time-honored and international tradition, Julio, the night watchman, was actually awake.

"Hello," he said with a genuinely warm smile.

"Hello," I replied, grimacing as I experienced another spasm. "I think I need a doctor," I managed through gritted teeth.

"Oh no, what's wrong?" he said, frowning sympathetically.

"I . . ." was all I could manage before, for the first time in my life, I collapsed in pain and then lay gasping on the ground.

I was vaguely aware when Julio helped me up, put me in a chair, and called a cab to take me to the local hospital.

"I finish in three hours," he said. "If you aren't back by then, I'll come and find you."

I didn't feel lonely anymore. I wanted to express my gratitude with a handshake, but instead I dropped to the ground again as he poured me into the taxi. I lay facedown against the cracked vinyl for the short trip to the hospital and then half-limped, half-staggered toward the emergency room, where a nurse seemed startled to see me.

Glancing in a mirror I saw an unfamiliar face. It was drawn and looked fifty-five, not thirty-five. Even more dire, it was surrounded by an appalling hairdo.

I'd had a birthday since coming to South America and at some stage had accidentally grown a mullet. The hair on top of my head had stopped growing as fast as the hair at the back some years before. Well, at least I was in the right country for such a travesty this time, as Argentinean men often have hairdos not even an eighties glam rocker would have contemplated.

A doctor soon came to examine me; he spoke no English and I spoke only a few words of Spanish. Mainly we used a mixture of pantomime and my idiotic way of speaking Spanish, which is to add an *o* to the end of English words. A surprising number of symptoms were covered in this manner before the doctor asked if I was suffering from diarrhea which, though far more sensibly spelled in Spanish, is pronounced the same way as in English.

"No," I replied in all honesty, though my answer was met with a cocked eyebrow.

"*Seguro?*" ("Are you sure?") he asked. A strange question, I thought. How could you *not* know?

I answered that I was sure, and he asked me again, and I realized his concern. "I'm not embarrassed!" I said, or at least tried to say, before recalling that *embarazada* means something entirely different and that I'd just wailed at the doctor that I wasn't "pregnant," something his medical training had presumably made evident to him.

The doctor left the room with a frown, and my homesickness returned. I couldn't believe that an empanada (or maybe several) had managed to do what Roy could not—put me in the hospital. My funds were low, cheap eats were all I could afford, yet my gut was mad as hell and not going to take it anymore.

Perhaps Patagonia was trying to kill me for failing to appreciate its charms. Was Friederike right? Was I too old and jaded? Or too old and pathetic for my body to withstand the insults it had shrugged off in my twenties?

The doctor returned with a needle that would have frightened a rhino and a painkilling tablet that looked more like a loaf than a pill. With little ceremony he jabbed the needle into my backside. Miraculously, within minutes, the writhing subsided, and soon I was feeling fine; in fact I felt so good by the time I made my way back through the hostel doors I *was* a little embarrassed. Anything that simple to cure shouldn't have needed a doctor, I felt, blushing as I thanked Julio.

"*De nada,*" he said.

I made my way back into the dorm room as first light seeped through the curtains, illuminating a disturbing sight of just how skimpy some Italian underwear is, and managed to sleep for an hour before the alarm to wake me for the Perito Moreno hike beeped rudely in my ear.

In that state of near drunkenness that sleeplessness can induce, I could scarcely recall the agony of the night before. I was excited. Finally I was going to see something special, I was sure of it.

And for once, I was right.

8

Blue World

I watched in wonder as a mini-van-size piece of ice dropped from the sheer face of the Perito Moreno glacier in front of us.

"That was huge!" I exclaimed, my voice a fractured crackle caused by lack of sleep.

"Not so big," one of the guides said.

A boat would lead us to the base of the Perito Moreno glacier, the sight of which had already stunned me into rare silence until the piece came off.

Within moments we had docked and a group of us began walking on a trail through a light forest. Sheer cliffs launched skyward to the left of us, delighting us with regular waterfalls that sprayed us as we passed. I caught some moisture on my tongue, tilting my head to do so and almost toppled backward.

A condor soared from over the ridgeline, and even though it was hundreds of feet overhead, the sheer enormity of its three-yard wingspan was staggering.

"Wow," I said, my wildlife-spotting grin already in full flight.

This was what I'd been searching for in Patagonia. Still grinning and lagging a little behind the group, I brushed my hands against lichen-heavy tree trunks, savoring the sensation of soft mosses underfoot. I caught up with the rest of the group gathered at a staging point where the guides were putting them into uncomfortable-looking harnesses that bulged in unflattering places and made all of us, even the women, look like we'd sprung a grand tumescence.

I was soon rigged up and then handed what looked like a grand inquisitor's ice skates. I've always thought *crampon* was one of the least attractive words, sounding like the bastard hybrid between something that invokes pain and an item men are mortified to buy on behalf of their wives. But crampons were essential here, as their jagged metal teeth would provide traction on the ice.

I teetered on the crampons and hesitantly stepped from the gravelly surface where we'd geared up onto the ice, immediately forgetting any concerns of balance or verticality as I soaked up the view in front of me. The glacier was inconceivably vast, stretching to the lake we'd come from to the right. To the left it was a chunky, corrugated, daunting mass of blue and white for miles, until it disappeared into mist, from the top of which poked snowcapped Andean peaks. This was so unlike the jungle-like, fetid South America of my days with Roy, and the surprise thrilled me.

If I'd done more research, I'd have known South America has the largest ice sheet outside the poles, and I might have had the foresight to pack some warmer clothes. I had thought that the light jersey I'd put on after my brief sleep would be adequate, but most in the group were wearing thick, Chewbacca-like coats.

"What makes the ice so blue?" an American woman asked the guide. On our way to the glacier, this particular woman had delayed us twice by getting lost in an area only twice the size of a shoebox, and my patience with her was wearing a little thin.

The color of the ice was so vivid it seemed like it could only be fake. I'd never seen such an intensity of blue outside of a butterfly's wing, but unlike the flash of blue from a tropical moth in a forest, this went on for miles.

"Smurf piss," I answered. She looked at me blankly for a long moment.

"The ice crystals are packed so densely that the only light that reflects off it is in the blue spectrum," our guide replied.

When I was a guide I might have run with the Smurf urine theory just to see how long people believed me, but this guy was apparently more professional than I had ever been.

"Here's something," another guide, a New Zealander, said as he hunched over something small and dark on the ice.

I clomped over, the crampon blades biting the ice with a crunch each step, and looked down to where he was pointing. Incongruous in this pristine environment, a turd sat starkly on the ice.

"Well, hello, Roy," I said. "You following me?"

"You name your poo Roy?" the guide asked.

"Um, no. It made me remember this puma named Roy I knew," I explained, then shut up.

In Africa I used to hear stories of leopards turning up in unexpected places (a sports stadium in Cape Town, the snow-capped summit of Kilimanjaro, and miles from shore on a small island in the middle of the vast Lake Kariba). The leopards' adaptability and ability to survive in any habitat was legendary. While the jaguars I sought might look like leopards, pumas were clearly this continent's real equivalent.

As we clomped deeper into the glacier, I concentrated on lifting my feet cleanly with each stride rather than engaging in a lazy shuffle. If I put the spikes on the crampons in the wrong place, I could be felled like a tree, hitting the lurid blue hard surface of the glacier face-first.

A slip and slide away from the carefully charted route the guides were taking us on could lead to any number of deathly chasms. The guides pointed out one of these, and the sheer scale of the glacier was shockingly apparent as I peered down a shaft of more than a hundred feet, at the base of which water rushed ferociously.

My fear of heights kicked in, and I was glad for the firm hold the New Zealand guide took on my belt.

"Easy mate," he said casually, and I realized I'd been swaying. With enormous concentration I lifted my clawed feet one by one and backed away from the hole.

We ate lunch soon after, some of us sitting on cloths that soon grew damp as the ice melted through them. Those who had brought plastic sheets probably felt smarter—until the heat made a slick layer underneath, causing them to toboggan forward into the nearest obstacle, which was usually someone sitting on a cloth.

After lunch we were allowed to wander on the glacier by ourselves. I split from the group and made my way over mounds of ice carved into sensual shapes by wind and water until I could see no one else. I paused and watched my breath plume out in front of me in short bursts. It had taken Roy four weeks to slim me down and get me fit, and I'd spent the last few weeks piling the weight back on. I was now markedly fatter and less fit than when I'd first come to South America.

I'd begun to find myself out of breath just at the thought of something strenuous. Like chewing. I probably needed to do something about it, I thought, then stopped myself with a mental slap. In the wild, experience and ability, rather than a svelte physique, are all that really matter.

I took in my surroundings. Around me was nothing but patterned ice, and I thought, *If I were left alone here, I would surely die.* It had been years since I'd felt this way, in the deserts of Namibia. It was exhilarating to feel this again.

In places where man is not dominant, but dwarfed and made feeble by nature, I get an adrenaline rush. My time with Roy had been a ride on a rollercoaster, but this was different. It was what I'd been missing for seven years. I promised myself never to let such a long gap happen again.

I pondered how my midlife fear of refrigerators had finally led me to South America, not because I am a thrill seeker, but because proximity to the kind of danger this place held made me feel alive. The feelings I had on the glacier were an unnameable concoction of awe, respect, gratitude, and even some kind of love. Contentment—that underrated emotion—was also present, but not for any good reason I could think of, given the danger. Right then, if I'd had a tail, I'd have wagged it.

Funnily enough I hadn't expected to feel like this here, having only felt it in places where animals might eat me, and— snobbishly, naively—I hadn't expected to experience it on a group tour. I realized my guides would probably scoff at such feelings, just as I had scoffed when people told me they were sure that some lion/elephant/sparrow gave them an aggressive look.

My reverie was interrupted by one of the guides who'd come to check that I hadn't fallen into a ravine.

"You okay?" he asked.

"Better than okay!" I shouted back.

Then it hit me. *Well I'll be,* I thought, surprised at myself when it hit me. *The place works!*

9

The Road from Patagonia

The Perito Moreno glacier turned out to be the high point of Patagonia; my next stop at El Chaten was pleasant enough, but unexciting. The rare and endangered deer species I had hoped to see had been as elusive as a park ranger had warned me, and the pumas he'd told me other tourists had seen were hidden too. Even the well-known mountain peaks stayed shrouded in fog.

El Chalten's bars were filled with glum-looking climbers, some of whom had been waiting weeks for the famously temperamental weather to clear enough for them to summit. I was amazed that any cloud could stay put in this wind, which was the strongest I'd seen in Patagonia. It shoved me around like a schoolyard bully, making me wonder if maybe I should join the climbers for a few beers and fatten up even more.

My next stop was Bariloche, a town with a bank. Historically it had not been considered part of Patagonia, but the town had lobbied successfully for tourism reasons—probably a bad sign—but it did have a museum solely dedicated to chocolate, something indicating an advanced culture at least.

The crowd that formed for the bus to Bariloche was made up of a near-perfect cross section of humanity. All continents, ages, colors, shapes, and heights were represented, even at the extremes. One was an extremely attractive, unusually tall blonde woman. I wished (not for the first time in my life) I had more confidence talking to strangers, especially the ones I found attractive.

Argentinean buses are remarkably punctual, and this one took off promptly at the time advertised. Within minutes we were chugging through spectacular mountain scenery, made all the more striking because the clouds had finally lifted. I could imagine the climbers at the bar raising their glasses one more time and bolting for the summit. At each sharp turn in the road, there was a small shrine containing statues of Mary and Jesus and colorful animal totems, marking the place where one or several vehicles had gone over the edge. These markers reflected a mix of Catholicism and the more ancient local traditions from a time well before the Incan dynasty.

As perturbing as the sheer number of these markers were, I was thrilled by the falcon-haunted cliffs, multicolored rock faces, and distant snowcaps.

Even with my face turned to the window most of the time, I spotted the tall blonde woman sitting a few rows back with an even taller man. I envied him, but noted they weren't talking. "Must be fighting," I thought, feeling a small rush of glee. Like many men of average or shorter height, I like it when men taller than me suffer.

After a while, the engine noises changed from a grumble to a purr, interrupted by the occasional rattle of an old and overworked machine. We had leveled out and abruptly left the mountains behind. The arid plain was so featureless that the world seemed nothing but horizon. Even though the dirt road was bullet straight and appeared silken smooth, the jiggling of our cheeks and chatter of our teeth revealed it was actually pitted and corrugated.

I can find beauty in the stark, and I appreciated the view outside as much as any other. Occasionally the flat stretches were interrupted by a glimpse of a distant lake in shades of the most impossible blue or deep green colors. These miraculous palettes were caused by glacial dust suspended in the water, which only allowed certain wavelengths of light to reflect. There were colorful shrines on this part of the road as well, though not as many. Judging by the slack, drooling mouths of the passengers around me, the flatness of the road had a soporific effect. I started checking periodically on the driver to make sure the bus's rocking wasn't acting as a lullaby for him too.

On the plus side, the beautiful tall woman still wasn't talking to the tall man, and the window's reflection afforded me a good view of the situation. Like most of us on the bus she was wearing bulky clothes to protect against the wind, but her high and defined cheekbones told me she was slender, and once again I envied the tall man, even though he was getting the silent treatment.

We stopped for lunch at a bedraggled store with a gutterless roof weighed down with stones, suggesting that the place saw lots of wind but little rain. The earth here was clearly poor, and all you could grow was despair. A sad-looking lamb near the store bleated at us, then sat beside an outdoor barbecue, as if aware of its eventual fate and more than ready to accept it.

When the bus continued on, the only feature outside was its shadow, expanding and contracting as we rocked from side to side. As night fell, we reached a one-taxi town with a few stores selling auto parts and gasoline and a single hotel run by a bear of a man and his three tiny daughters, all under ten, all working behind the bar. Part of the cost of the bus ticket was accommodations, and I was billeted to a shared room. A slightly built German man from the bus smiled heartily at me. Though clearly from a place where dentistry wasn't in vogue, he was very friendly and spoke perfect English. We spent at least five minutes arguing over who should have the larger of the three beds in the room before agreeing to leave it for whoever else was sharing with us.

The door opened, and it was the tall woman's even taller boyfriend.

"Where's your girlfriend?" the German and I asked almost simultaneously in Spanish, and I wondered if my toothy roommate had had to share rooms with couples whose sense of discretion was no match for their randiness.

"I don't have a girlfriend," he replied, the look on his face conveying his distaste for having to share a room with two crazy midgets.

He was French. Our only common language was a patchwork of Spanish. The tall woman was a stranger to him, and they'd hardly exchanged a word all day. He did not know her name or where she was from.

Interesting, I mused. Now if only I could think of something to say to her.

■ ■

At six the next morning, three alarms in our room began ringing, and three weary fists rubbed sleep from six weary eyes before we all politely argued over who should use the bathroom first. The Frenchman's bladder won.

Within minutes we were waiting for the bus, then were told to wait some more. Then some more. Eventually we were herded onto two buses, the second of which I landed on. I watched the first bus peel away before hearing ours splutter, fart, and then gurgle so wretchedly it was clearly the sound of something breathing its last.

"The bus is not fixed," our driver said in Spanish, which I thought was quite a clever observation.

Herded back off the bus, we waited some more and watched the driver and a local mechanic's legs for half an hour. I noticed that the tall-good-looking-woman-who-didn't-have-a-French-boyfriend had not gotten on the luckier bus. I grasped for something to say, something impressive, rejected all options, and harrumphed at my shyness as she walked far enough away that my only way of getting close would render me terrier-like in pursuit.

The legs moved little from their position jutting out under the bus until a voice shouted, "Bravo!" from underneath and the mechanic and driver emerged with greasy grins and triumphant eyes.

We clambered back on, and I noticed that the tall blonde woman was seated immediately behind me.

"Bloody hell, if we don't move soon we'll never get there," said an Australian behind me.

It wasn't the good-looking-tall-woman-without-the-French-boyfriend, but the woman in the seat next to her.

A common accent is a good pretext to introduce yourself, and I swapped names with the Australian. Ange and I soon figured out we were both from Sydney. The tall blonde woman looked out the window, occasionally flicking her eyes toward Ange and me as we chatted. She looked Nordic, I decided. She probably had that enviable Scandinavian ability of casually speaking half a dozen languages, which automatically makes you feel like a poor citizen of the world because you don't.

Conversation with Ange came to a lull, and I returned to the view outside.

"Armadillo!" I shouted happily some time later, startling all around me except the frustratingly impassive tall blonde sans French boyfriend. She continued staring out the window.

The animal I had seen had dashed away from our looming tires and dived into a culvert, so I was left in the awkward position of explaining that I had indeed seen it. I glanced at the blonde, wondering why she was so aloof, then saw the telltale trail of headphone cords in her hair.

Doofus! I said to myself.

We didn't get far before the bus began a series of hopping lurches. The driver managed to coax it on a few more miles to a service station, where we were instructed simply to get off the bus and wait.

It could have been frustrating, but years in Africa had taught me that impatience only gets you wrinkles, so it's best to make what you can from such a situation. We were at least liberated from the confines of bus seats as wide as toothpicks and about as comfortable to put your buttocks on.

Finally I grew frustrated with my own shyness, and sadly without a plan I sidled closer to the tall blonde who didn't have a French boyfriend, keen to impress but with little to offer in the way of witty banter. I decided to stick to the one subject I can talk confidently about and cast about for an animal.

Fortunately for me one was nearby, and as I watched it, it began to do something I recognized and could impressively interpret. "Oh look!" I exclaimed. "That cat's about to puke!" Often animals defy prediction, but this one backed me up and vomited profusely.

"Um, thanks for showing me that," she said, blinking.

"You're English?" I said, startled not to hear a Nordic lilt.

"Welsh actually," she said.

I mentally kicked myself. I felt I should have known the difference.

"But both my parents are English," she added, "so my accent is a bit mixed up."

This little bit of self-deprecation—which absolved me for being ignorant *and* an imperialist—made my burgeoning crush crank up a notch. It ratcheted up further as our conversation drifted and she mentioned she was also a rugby fan. "And Wales is the best team in the world," she announced.

"Ranked about sixth officially, though, aren't they?" I said.

She gave me a withering look. Right. *Be polite to the beautiful woman,* I reminded myself. My seven years in a relationship before I left Australia had clearly left my flirtation skills a little rusty.

I really wanted whatever I said next to be at least correct, if not impressive, so I thrust my hand out as if at a business meeting and said, "My name's Peter."

"Lisa," she replied, shaking my hand with a slight smirk. She thought I was incredibly awkward, I could tell.

"Nice name," I said, then felt flustered that maybe I was being too complimentary, so I changed the subject. "But I think I will call you 'the Minke,'" I announced.

Lisa glossed right over whether it was appropriate to nickname someone you'd just met after an enormous mammal and instead simply asked me why.

A smarter person would have stayed quiet and denied ever having said such a thing, but I replied, "Because you're from Wales."

Having revealed myself as a fool, I should have stopped digging deeper into the hole, but instead out of nervousness I added, "And because you're big."

I gulped, tasting the feet I had in my mouth.

The Minke smiled.

"That's pretty odd," she said, "but I like it!"

Wow, I thought, *that's amazing.* I hadn't meant the name as an insult (to me no animal name is an insult), but many women would not be as graceful in being called an animal weighing several tons. (At least I hadn't called her Humpback.) My little crush grew like a plankton bloom, and I resolved to be cool and not make any more references to sea creatures.

I kept my resolution with respect to the sea creatures and didn't bring up the subject of cat vomit again, but cool eluded me. When we were finally allowed back on the bus, I soon developed neck strain from constantly turning around to talk to Lisa.

To make matters worse, the bus came to a juddering halt. Our driver leapt from the vehicle as if it were in flames and ran into the gravel plain by the side of the bus. Something scuttled ahead of him, jigging as he jagged, but with nowhere to hide in this featureless landscape.

"Armadillo!" I shouted again delightedly, though I immediately became concerned about how it would be treated. The armadillo's frantic movement finally ceased when the driver pinned the animal with his foot, which looked harsh but probably wasn't that bad given all the armor armadillos wear. I thought about telling the driver that armadillos are susceptible to leprosy, but I lacked the ability to say, "Keep touching that and parts may well begin to drop off you," in Spanish.

I exited the bus with a few others, including the Minke, to get a better look, Squinting in the sandblasting wind, I looked at the little creature being pinned to the ground by a booted foot and wondered how far I would go to set it free.

To my relief the driver did not keep the animal for the cooking pot, but instead let the armadillo go, and it scooted off into the horizon, puffs of dust spurting from its tiny feet as it went. Perhaps the bus driver was only trying to let his passengers actually see an armadillo rather than relying on my poky reports. We all got back on the bus, and Lisa told me she was delighted to have seen it. "Armadillo!" she said. "Crunchy on the outside, soft on the inside!"

Seeing my hesitant grin she added, "You don't get it do you?"

"Nope," I replied, relieved, and liking her goofiness.

"Why don't you explain it over dinner if we all go out tomorrow," suggested Ange (now an angel in my mind). I could have kissed her, but worried that it might send a mixed signal.

■ ■

The next few hours ticked by quite easily in conversation with Lisa and Ange, and I found out that Lisa had been traveling a few months already, but had come from the other side of the continent, through Brazil before Argentina.

"Was that daunting by yourself?" I asked.

"No," she replied. "Daunting was Paraguay. I went there to see the world's least visited world heritage site." Just my kind of lunatic quest.

She continued, "I found out no one goes there because it is pretty crappy. Scary country, too. It's the only place where I have felt unsafe so far." I felt the urgent need to offer some sort of protection, should she want it, for the rest of her travels. This urge would be ridiculous for its chest-thumping masculinity alone, and even more so because she was bigger than I was and clearly quite capable of taking care of herself. For once I kept quiet.

As we approached Bariloche, there was a dramatic shift in scenery and afterward a small dip that didn't seem to signify anything of great note. Pine trees appeared outside, along with many other forms of unfamiliar vegetation. Soon after, clusters of lights in the distance announced our arrival on the outskirts of Bariloche.

A pensive mood overtook me after I'd exited the bus. I had dinner plans to look forward to, and Lisa really seemed like she might like me. But Patagonia had not been what I'd expected. I probably could have searched more of it for the sense of isolation I had been promised, and maybe I would have found it outside of the glacier, but not without a far-larger budget. The bus driver's interaction with the armadillo seemed to represent the Patagonia I'd seen—once wild, but now held down and subdued. Instead of seeing an untamed Patagonia, I was yet another pair of human feet domesticating it.

An Argentinean woman with a flush-faced baby was waiting for a bus that would take her the way we had just come. There was something odd about the baby. I realized that its cheeks were not merely ruddy, but already blotched, blasted, and burned, not by sun but by the abrasive air. The baby didn't look unhappy, but it must be difficult to be so small and suffer such insults to your skin. I had sympathy, as I could already feel a cold sore developing that would eventually take the same shape as Italy, and be almost the same size.

The cold sore and the baby's ruddy cheeks meant the same thing. Patagonia could not be fully domesticated. They might build roads through it, catch every armadillo, and put a trinket store on every corner. But the place could never be tamed while that wind blew, and that thought made my cracked lips crease into a painful smile.

10

The Joy of Pessimism

Over steaks and malbec, Argentina's signature wine, Lisa and I discovered that our travel plans overlapped in many places. Ange chaperoned us for one night and then returned to Australia—perhaps she was the exception that proved my rule about Australians and their aversion to long plane rides, because her visit to South America had been fairly short.

One thing I love about travel is making changes on a whim, and with my interest in Lisa somewhat stronger than a whim, I was delighted when she agreed to us merging travel routes for as long as it pleased us. "Do you really not mind me calling you 'the Minke'?" I asked one day. I loved calling her that, but at times I feared she was just tolerating the nickname.

"No, I really do like it! But you can use my real name at times if you can remember it."

"Of course I do." I paused, as if dredging my memory. "Ailsa? No, that's not it. Alisa? No, close, I'm sure . . ." and she gave me a playful wallop, and while thrilled at the touch, I was also startled by her reach. If she did become my girlfriend, as I hoped, I was very glad that I was a runner, not a fighter (a philosophy that would be tested later in my journey).

■ ■

Lisa and I made our way across Bolivia and into Brazil to the town of Miranda as just travel companions, and there met a burly man with the strong, angular features of the region's indigenous people. His name was Marcello, and he was passionate about the very animal I so wanted to see: the jaguar.

I decided I liked Marcello, for the strange reason of how he killed a chicken. We were on the fringes of the Pantanal, a famous wetland often compared to my beloved Okavango Delta in Botswana and a haven for wildlife of all sorts. We'd come there to see the astonishing birds it was known for, as well as capybaras (the world's largest rodent, a guinea pig that weighs more than a supermodel), alligators, and tapirs. The Pantanal is also famous for jaguars.

Marcello had been recommended to us as a man who knew the Pantanal but also had an affinity for the big cat I sought. He was intrigued by my guiding background, and as we drove from Miranda into the wetlands, we swapped stories of lunatic tourists before reverting to what we both loved most. Initially I thought maybe he was pretending he loved animals as part of his customer service, but then I saw him kill a chicken.

He was driving us on a tarred road, and the few cars we encountered were traveling fast. Sugar cane grew high on either side of the road, and from the tight clusters of it a scraggly looking chicken decided to cross the road at the exact same time an oncoming vehicle appeared. To swerve around the chicken would mean a head-on collision, so Marcello held his course, and there was a deathly thump under the vehicle.

"I'm so sorry," Marcello said. "So sorry," he repeated, and I could see his brown knuckles go a shade paler from gripping the wheel so tightly. Maybe he wasn't apologizing to Lisa and me, maybe it was to the chicken, but I could see a real tear in his eye. This was exactly the sort of guide I wanted.

Marcello knew my aim—to see a jaguar in the wild while ticking off as many other species feathered and furred along the way as I could.

"It is not the right season," he said, "but you never know."

I'd said exactly the same thing over the years to tourists who hoped to see some elusive bird or animal, and I knew he was right. You do never know. Jaguars tend not to migrate, but in this drier season they had more open land to roam in and thus were harder to find. I was feeling lucky.

While we were in Miranda, Lisa and I had met Marcello's wife, plus his three dogs, including a puppy he had just rescued from a somber fate. The puppy's mother had been poisoned, and she had died by the water's edge. A type of alligator called a caiman had appreciated the easy meal, and had already taken all but one of her mourning puppies before Marcello grabbed the sole survivor.

Lisa had become enamored with the puppy, and I think she was just as happy seeing him as she would be any jaguar. But before we even tried to meet a jaguar, almost impossible in the heat of the day, we would meet the orphan-making caiman.

"It's huge!" Marcello said. "Huge!" he reiterated. "At least eight feet!"

I almost snorted in a way that would have revealed my wildlife snobbery. Both Australia and Africa have crocodiles at least twice the size of a human, with records of over twenty feet in both places. But I withheld my snort when I considered that since our plan was to swim with it, eight feet was more than huge enough.

"It was right there," said Marcello, indicating the spot with a machete he kept holstered on his belt at all times, perhaps even when he slept. "Huge!" he said again. I recognized the love of animals again in his enthusiasm—even his sympathy for the puppy didn't dampen his excitement.

Soon we were in a lagoon formed to the side of a gently flowing stream. We paddled around, Marcello explaining that the caiman was curious and would often bob to the surface and slowly approach, getting as close as a foot away, a distance from which there was no chance of escape should it get nippy. There were also piranhas in the water, but I was less nervous about them. I had read that despite their reputed voraciousness for meat, most piranhas are primarily vegetarian. They scavenge for already-dead meat on occasion, and only if trapped in a shrinking pool turn into savage flesh-tearing nightmares.

We paddled around. I even went into the deeper water, but the caiman didn't show, and it occurred to me that if it had recently eaten a poisoned dog it might not be in the best of health. Then again, reptiles have digestive systems that can handle almost anything.

This was our first bust. No sign of a caiman. No nip from a piranha. But as we came out of the water, Marcello pointed to a tree down the road that he said we should check out.

The tree had four parallel scratches down it, deep into the bark. This was territorial marking, something I was used to from the jaguar's African cousin, the leopard. But these were widely spaced, and high up. The animal that had made these *was* huge, almost the size of a female lion.

"Huge!" Marcello said, echoing my thoughts. I wondered if he thought most animals qualified for this adjective.

We drove on from the swimming spot, and I noted with some regret just how many roads there were in the area. The construction of roads that disturb wetlands is bad enough. But roads bring not just tourists like Lisa and me but also poachers. Marcello stopped the car, and we homed in on vultures we had seen circling, then dropping, to a point not far from the road.

It turned out the target of the vultures was a caiman, this one no threat to us because of a bullet hole to its skull and a hacked-off tail. Much of the meat was missing, and Marcello said the poachers would sell it to restaurants.

We stood in a respectful silence, like mourners at a funeral, with no need to voice our disgust. "Shame," said Marcello, breaking the silence. "He was huge."

A bit sobered from the experience, we drove back to the camp, showered, and prepared for an afternoon boat ride, which could provide good jaguar spotting, because they often sun themselves on riverbanks. I felt a tingle of anticipation.

The atmosphere was as electric as the eels in the water around us. One briefly swam to the surface, unusual in daylight hours, and despite my lunatic compulsion to grab it to see just how strong the shock would be, I resisted. They produced enough voltage to stop your heart, I had read. When I mentioned the urge, Lisa just shook her head at my strange curiosity and said, "I keep worrying that I am going to have to write an e-mail to your sister saying, 'Dear Laurie, we've never met, but I thought I should pass on some bad news . . .'"

"People here fear these eels more than the piranhas," Marcello explained. "It is only your movies that make people think piranhas are bad." No more swimming in this part of the river, I decided. It was time to focus on land creatures, particularly jaguars.

I tried to dampen the enthusiasm I was feeling. For years I've believed that pessimists are the happiest people on Earth, because they're never disappointed and have many more pleasant surprises than starry-eyed optimists. I also believe that anticipation is often greater than reward. Still, I remained sure that seeing a jaguar would be more thrilling than I had ever imagined.

That afternoon my bird count advanced at the pace of a child chasing an ice-cream truck. Everywhere we looked, there were bloat-throated Jabiru storks stabbing at catfish, scarlet ibis spattered pink as if they had been inexpertly painted, wonderful Toco toucans with absurd banana beaks, and Mardi Gras–colored macaws. Unfortunately a jaguar failed to materialize, making me wonder if I needed to have the tingle I'd been feeling checked out by a nurse.

That night we ate freshly caught fish from the river and slurped thirstily at icy cold beers before moving onto caipirinhas. This Brazilian specialty is a delicious sweet-and-sour cocktail that insists you have more than one. We obeyed and were soon rollicking with laughter at each other's stories. Marcello had a bounty of jaguar tales, and I countered with stories of elephants and lions. With some guides the swapping of stories might have become competitive, but ours was just easy banter, and Lisa seemed to find it funny, even though by now she'd heard most of my stories before. I'd tried to impress her by emphasizing my decade-old adventures, glossing over my recent years of desk work in Sydney.

After a while I found myself asking Marcello what it was he loved about guiding.

"I love the Pantanal," he said, with a resigned shrug. "I want others to love it, too."

I understood. I felt the same way about Africa's wild places. But the next thing he described was something I had never experienced.

"I was born here, a real Indian, in a tribe that lived in those hills that I showed you. I don't even know how old I am, because we had no watches or calendars. We just hunted, fished, and lived with the animals, like animals."

I was surprised to hear him say they lived like animals, then considered that maybe it was only in our culture that such a thing would be considered unflattering. Such a strong link to a place was something I could not comprehend—being a nomad might be about gaining experiences, but that was one I could never have. For a moment I envied Marcello his deep, deep roots, so different from my ambivalence toward my place of birth. He belonged here in a way that I couldn't belong anywhere, and much as I love being nomadic, I envied that.

But then Marcello continued, "Sometimes we would meet outsiders, but mostly we tried to avoid them. All they wanted was to take," he said, then paused. "Then some diamond miners came and wanted what was under our land." He paused again, longer this time, and took a long sip from his drink. I signaled the barman, and he began crushing limes for another round.

"My people didn't want the mine, so the miners attacked us," Marcello continued, and I felt like I knew what was coming, and that everything had changed from casual conversation to the stuff of tragedy. "They tied us up and then attacked my mother. My father got free and ran to help her, so they shot him. Then they shot my mother." Marcello's face was scrunched and red, and a tear fell.

"I ran away, and kept running," he continued. "I never went back. Some days later, I was found on a farm by some people who took me in. It was in the papers, that an Indian had been found on a farm, but I couldn't tell anyone what had happened because nobody spoke my language.

"I worked on the farm of the people who found me, and they adopted me, teaching me Portuguese. Then one day a neighbor had some tourists on his farm. He had heard that I was good at finding animals, so I helped with the tourists, and that is how I started guiding, learning English and some German, too."

"You were very lucky that those people found you and took you in," Lisa said.

Marcello shrugged. "Yes ... but they used to beat me. So much."

Lisa and I both rocked back in our chairs, horrified.

Marcello's broad shoulders shook with some suppressed memory. "I want a daughter," he said suddenly, "because they don't get distracted like men do to chase money and women, and she will learn languages so she can speak to everyone, and I will teach her to be the best guide in the Pantanal and show all these idiots how to do it. They don't love the Pantanal; they just want the tips. I want a daughter to do what I do. That would make a good future for this place."

"You're an optimist," I said, leaving it at that, but wanting to commend him after all the hardships he had faced.

"What else can you be?" he asked.

Later that night Lisa and I wended our way along a straight path. "I really feel any complaints I have about life are petty," Lisa said.

"Me too," I agreed, and could add no more, feeling chastened about any thoughts I'd ever had that my life was hard, and flattered that Marcello shared his intimate stories. I was driven to protect animals because they mattered to me. Marcello had a sense of ownership, kinship even, that I could only grasp at but never hold. Perhaps I needed to partake of some of Marcello's philosophies. As we reached the door to our rooms, I borrowed some of Marcello's optimism, took Lisa's hand, and pulled her close. She was a full head taller than I was, but felt light, as if made of bird's wings. Then I leaned up and kissed her.

11

There Is a Jaguar, Right Here!

The next morning we set out again by boat. This time we were joined by two Germans who may have wondered why I couldn't stop smiling. We went well away from areas used by other tourists and casual fishers. The Pantanal was again vibrant with birds, and howler monkeys high in the tree tops blended well with their surrounds, despite their shiny red fur. Despite being "delicious" as Marcello told us they were and thus prone to being hunted, many capybaras lazed by the banks, looking remarkably content as the sun's first rays warmed them.

We stopped at an island at the center of myriad intersecting channels and set up there for the day. Marcello had seen a female jaguar's tracks a few days earlier, and felt that she might have come this way. The two Germans were just as keen as I was, so we set off eagerly on a trail, picking our footing carefully but nevertheless managing to tread on every crackly leaf, every snapping twig, while Marcello's broad and bare feet moved noiselessly over the forest floor.

I scanned the ground for tracks, yet saw nothing but the hippo-like splayed toe marks of capybara, the pads and claw marks of some smaller predator that I couldn't identify—maybe a raccoon species—and a fox's clear marks, but no large cat. Marcello's head moved from side to side, up and down, as trackers do, but he also found nothing to indicate he'd been right about the jaguar.

It was another bust, but the locale was so idyllic that I couldn't feel disappointment. The boatman had strung up hammocks while we walked, and we lazed in these under the shade of canopied trees while he cooked us a lunch of more fresh fish, the river flowing gently by mere feet away. After eating we returned to more lazing, I felt the need for a swim.

I wandered upstream to an open section of bank, the muddy trail to it dense with capybara tracks. I waded in, feeling a current far stronger than the mellow surface had led me to believe. Lisa joined me, and in a sheltered, slow flowing section of channel we splashed at each other, and I made a motion to chase her. In a few strokes she was so far ahead of me that my pursuit was clearly ridiculous, her long limbs propelling her at a pace I had no chance of matching. Like most Australians I am confident in the water, but her ease at outswimming me stripped away some of my assurance and put a small dent in my ego. Lisa had told me that she'd represented her country in swimming in the European championships, so I shouldn't have been surprised, nor as concerned when she swam straight into the strongest part of the current and was swept away.

"Minke?" I called after her. "You okay?"

Overhanging foliage and the channel's curve obscured my view, and I had no idea how far she had gone.

"Fine," she said casually, stroking back into view with clear ease, a feat I knew would leave me panting and close to cardiac arrest if I tried it. She let the current take her again, and once more was lost to my sight.

But there was something else in the water. Close to the bank opposite me, a dark head appeared, then another beside it. They were only thirty feet from me, but it took me some moments to establish what I was seeing. Then two more heads appeared, and one looked directly at me, its sleek head swiveling on a submerged neck, its dark brown eyes expressionless as it took me in.

"Giant otters!" I shouted gleefully, heedless of having berated tourists for doing the same thing over the years. But the otters ignored me. The largest of the otter family, giant otters can weigh up to eighty pounds, and while they look cute, they can be aggressively territorial and vicious in the defense of their young.

I felt confident I would not be any sort of threat and did an inelegant flop into deeper water, feeling the tug of the flow immediately. My plan had been to swim across to the other side where the otters were holding almost still, with no visible effort backstroking into the current.

Angling into the flow my energy was soon sapped, and the otters with the most casual flick of their tails took off downstream, their heads bobbing lightly as if laughing at my feebleness. With no hope of catching up to them, I turned to go back, only to see the bank rapidly disappearing. I stroked to the side, but it was a mess of tangled vegetation and I was wary of snags that could trap an ankle and pull me under.

Something stroked my belly, most likely a branch, but at this speed something like that could cut me deeply, and that would surely be enough to excite piranhas out of their vegetarianism. Feeling foolish, and wondering once again why I always felt so compelled to get close to animals, I made cautious backward strokes to slow myself before I hit our aluminum boat at ramming speed, generating a resonant *DONG* from its hull.

"*Tutto bong?*" the boat driver asked me as I clutched the boat side, trying desperately to look cool while gasping like a dying goldfish.

"*Tutto bong,*" I replied, two of the only words I knew in Portuguese, which meant "All okay."

"You just hit the boat, didn't you?" Lisa asked from the hammock she'd managed to get into with far less difficulty and infinitely more grace than I'd managed as I'd exited the water.

"Maybe," I said sheepishly.

Despite my misadventure, I decided to leave the others to their hammocks and dry off by going for a walk alone in the forest near our picnic sight. Parrots squabbled in overhead branches, their green a perfect match for the leaves, while green and orange rufous-tailed jacamars sallied forth from low perches to nab damselflies. An agouti, the smaller and daintier cousin of the capybara, picked its way delicately through some undergrowth nearby. Life was everywhere, but no jaguars—not even a sign of them. Nevertheless I felt relaxed in the forest in a way most people describe being at a beach, and I only reluctantly made my way back to the group, figuring we would push back into the current soon.

We had a lazy, wonderful afternoon puttering on the river, and as dusk set in we came to a place that Marcello's instinct said would be good for jaguar spotting. Once again, anticipation took hold of me no matter how I resisted it, the relaxed mood I had been in dispatched as swiftly as the sun.

We beached the boat on a muddy bank with tangled, looping vegetation, the gaps between branches just wide enough to limbo through. Still barefoot, Marcello led us quietly along the bank, then held up his hand for us to stop. My pulse ratcheted up at the sight in front of us, and I held my breath.

Clear in the mud in front of us were the tracks of a big cat and a smoothed patch of ground where the cat had lain down. The edges were sharp, and no insect tracks crossed these marks, a certain indicator of freshness in this life-filled place. A jaguar had been here only moments before. I breathed out, puffing my cheeks as I did, not wanting to get too excited.

"Look there!" whispered Marcello, suddenly pointing, and my pulse shot up again. But there was no jaguar, just more tracks— not just the tracks of an adult but two smaller sets as well.

"She's got babies!" Marcello whispered to us.

I was excited, but then my heart sank. It gets dark suddenly in the tropics, as sudden as the flicking of a switch, and following a jaguar in prime hunting hours would be beyond dangerous. Add to this a mother with cubs, and even I would have vetoed any idea of trying to approach them on foot. Marcello clearly agreed, and with hand gestures indicated that we should back away until we reached the boat.

"Is there a way around?" I asked with a desperate hope in my voice.

Marcello pondered, then slowly shook his head. "Not here, not now. We can try farther along in the car later tonight. Maybe they will come out."

■ ■

That night we bundled into Marcello's four-wheel drive, and with flashlights splayed from each window and a spotlight mounted at the front, drove along the roads in the area. Capybaras glared at us, moving off the road at the last possible moment; a crab-eating fox trotted gaily along in front of us before scurrying into the brush; and a raccoon with some sort of prey in its mouth crossed our beams, but sadly no jaguar emerged.

I was wired with suspense that night and barely slept, excited to have been so close to seeing a jaguar and frustrated to have missed out.

The next day Lisa and I had to move on. We were now traveling as a couple. My pessimism in the past has led to accusations that I'm a cynic, but right then I must have been one of the most optimistic people in the world. Our time with Marcello had been spectacular, so I was in no way disappointed, and I was sure there was a jaguar for me somewhere down the dirt tracks of South America.

12

8.8

I'd been traveling almost six months when Lisa and I decided to return to my friends in Santiago. I was broke and waiting for a payment that was due, so we spent more than a week in Santiago, a city occasionally reviled by travelers but unfairly so. While it lacks the exuberance of Buenos Aires or sexiness of Rio it has its charms, many of which never appear in guidebooks for reasons known only to their authors. Lisa too was happy to have a brief break from life on the road.

Marguerite and Harris's house was a relatively private setting in which we could explore our new relationship. Among the goofy smiles and excessive hand-holding in a relationship's early stages is something more daunting, and far less pleasant. This was the first time we would share a bathroom. I am thrilled whenever a woman finds me attractive, and I felt the need to preserve that with Lisa. So it was with some force that I prevented Lisa from brushing her teeth soon after I had left the room.

"Why can't I go in?" she asked.

I had no reasonable answer, so I said, "It's haunted."

"What?"

"Okay, not haunted, but does smell like something is dead in there."

"You're a fool," she replied, pushing past me, and I had an inkling it wouldn't be the last time she said that.

Neither Lisa's opinion of me nor her experience with how I could befoul a bathroom scared her off completely. My turn came when we went to a local bar solely to watch her beloved Welsh rugby team play France. During the game Lisa screamed at the screen, shook her fists, and generally scared the small cluster of French fans into a cautious silence.

Holy crap. My girlfriend is a guy, I thought, but didn't dare say it. My opinion didn't change when Wales's defeat spurred her to drown her sorrows with copious amounts of liquor. Not even my steel-plated liver could keep up, so I didn't try.

At 3:34 the next morning, I woke, feeling disoriented and confused by a noise I'd never heard before and a world out of control. I grabbed the Minke and insisted she get out of bed.

"I've been through worse!" she insisted, and rolled over, the mattress bouncing as she did. The whole house was behaving like a bull with an unwanted rider on its back. The window panes strained against their frames with violent pulsations, and somewhere I could hear waves, incongruous this far from the coast. Later I realized it was the in-ground swimming pool. The earthquake had thrown half of its contents onto the surrounding lawn.

With Lisa reluctantly upright, we staggered toward the bathroom doorframe. A wall came from nowhere and bounced us to the side, then the other jabbed us and pushed us back. "We're being beaten up by a house!" I cried.

"I'm going back to bed!" Lisa slurred.

"No, no, let's just get into the doorway," I said, dragging her.

"Now you *want* me to go to the bathroom!" Lisa complained. At the doorway I bullied her, still complaining, against the frame and stood panting from the effort and adrenaline. We were on the second floor of the house, and I could see no way of us surviving if the house collapsed, something that seemed inevitable as the quake continued.

Later I would learn that the quake had lasted just over forty seconds, but at the time it felt like an eon. I believed that standing in the doorway was our best option for safety and slyly figured anything falling would land on the Minke before me anyway. I also learned after the quake that standing in doorways may not be the best strategy for surviving an earthquake. Rescuers often find survivors near beds or tables where, if the ceiling collapses, it hits the object first and then angles over the person in a kind of "triangle of life."

"I'm going out to check on the others," I said. Lisa, who was either still drunk or still suicidally forlorn over her rugby team's loss, replied, "I'm going back to bed." And she did, maintaining a far straighter line to it than she had to the doorway.

I heard voices in the hallway and found the entire Gomez family—Harris, Marguerite, and their five-year-old daughter and six-month-old baby, gathered in various states of pyjamery outside the cluster of bedrooms that made up the house's upper floor.

"Why is the house driving?" the five-year-old asked, a beautiful summation of the grinding pulses we had just felt. Marguerite had moist eyes, and I could see she was still shaking. Harris asked after Lisa, and I explained she was back in bed.

"She's tough," said Harris, eyebrows raised in admiration.

"Drunk actually, but how are all of you?" I replied.

Everyone was fine, and Harris and I went off to check for damage to the house. The electricity was out, and the view from the window stunned us both into silence. The house had been built on the side of a dormant volcano and overlooked a valley into central Santiago. Usually the city winked and sparkled; now there was nothing but the occasional red flare of an emergency light. There was nothing to indicate whether the city of seven million people still stood—or had fallen. In the gloom around us all that was clear was that a neighbor's house was still upright, but it was impossible to know what was happening beyond that.

Sirens went off, one by one, and far below some headlights wended their way in a serpentine fashion that made me think they could only be avoiding rubble. Later I learned that many of the lights I saw were people hastily making their way home to loved ones—it was a Friday night after all, and Latinos start partying late and finish even later.

It occurred to me that I should find out if I could be of help to anyone.

"What do you think is going on out there?" Harris asked.

"No idea," I replied honestly, wishing there was more light but feeling sure we would be without electricity for some time. There would be death out there, I knew, but who knew how much. A quake had claimed more than one hundred thousand lives in Haiti quite recently, and I hoped it would be nothing like that. Santiago is far wealthier and hopefully more solidly built. Images from that disaster made me worry about looters. The Gomezes are financially comfortable, and I feared the very worst in human nature beyond the walls of this house. As Harris and I trudged to the upper level of the house, I decided that the top of the stairs would be our best line of defense should anyone break in.

I lay awake for several hours after I went back to bed. Suddenly there was a sound like an angry ocean, and a second later the house began to shake again. Once again, the windows flexed far more than I thought glass could, and the bed bounced as if a giant was jumping on it.

"I felt that one," Lisa said, waking.

"Hard not to," I replied, and again went into the hall.

"Not as big as the first," Harris said.

"Nope. Don't think so," I replied.

"How many more will there be?" Marguerite asked.

I had no idea. Santiago sits right on the junction between two tectonic plates. In 1960 it had experienced the most powerful earthquake ever recorded, one so devastating that most of the city had to be rebuilt. What I learned later was that Chile had subsequently instituted one of the world's strictest building codes, and actually adhered to it. But looking over the darkened valley it was impossible to know how successful they had been. Only dawn would tell.

Tremors came throughout the night, some powerful enough to push the pool water around again, triggering howls from every neighborhood dog, except my hosts' loafing cocker spaniel, who just ignored the entire affair.

With light came the discovery that not only the Gomezes but all of their neighbors had been spared serious harm. Apart from broken glass and zigzagging cracks in roads, there was no damage of note. Only later would we find out that some of the few buildings that had survived the 1960 quake had been unable to take a second blow.

Within six hours of the initial quake, the electricity was back on. The Internet took only twelve hours. The local supermarket stayed closed a day as the staff put everything that had fallen off the shelves back on (I imagined them watching forlornly as aftershocks toppled them off again), and the ATMs all ran out of money as people made panic withdrawals. Nevertheless by Monday it was all systems go. I had often faced greater inconveniences in Africa with no earthquakes involved.

The media, though, was painting a very different picture. While we knew that the world outside the window was secure, it was hard to get reliable information about other places the quake may have hit. We gathered around the television as soon as the power was back on and were immediately told that Santiago was in flames, the city destroyed, and as bad as that sounded, Concepcion to the south was even worse.

"They're pretty much saying we are dead," I said. "I feel fine though."

It was the worst sort of sensationalist reporting. Concepcion, it was true, was far worse hit than the capital, but Santiago got a black eye and was never knocked down. Footage showed the army beating a looter stealing a television, but close observation showed that a woman behind taking bread from a supermarket was given free passage. No one resented that.

Contrary to what the news reported, Santiago was not in ruins. I began to see a national spirit that I had never seen anywhere else before. Chileans rallied to help their fellow countrymen, in ways small and large. Cars were painted with the slogan FUERZA CHILE! (Strength Chile), and teenagers were at work in supermarkets, asking customers if they would buy items for people in need such as milk formula or canned food that could be donated outside for distribution. Normally if there is any animal that I would claim to dislike, it is my own species, but I found myself with a permanent lump in my throat to see so much solidarity.

■ ■

Two weeks after the earthquake, Lisa's parents, at her urging, came to visit. We all felt the best way we could help was to put money into the economy and let others know that Chile was dealing with the problem better than an outsider might imagine. We drove Lisa's parents along the Pan American Highway, Chile's major artery, and saw sights that staggered her father, who as an engineer was able to properly appreciate how well roads and buildings had withstood the violence and how quickly infrastructure was being tended to.

"I don't believe it," Papa Minke said as we drove along, "I've never seen that in the U.K.!"

I scanned around for things I imagined would be unfamiliar to Brits, such as a shower or a winning sports team, but saw none.

"There were four guys standing in a hole there, and instead of just one guy working and three 'supervising,' all four had shovels and were hard at it!" he explained.

I had to agree it was impressive and unusual. This trip was making me shed even more cynicism about the human animal. In the wrecked town of Linares we witnessed the greatest destruction wrought by the earthquake. Adobe houses had tumbled to the ground, and the church's steeple was far from plumb, skewed as it was into the main roof of the building. But there was no wailing, just hard work going on. There was nowhere to stay in Linares, so we bought some supplies there and headed on until we reached Chillan. It took some searching, but we found a small hostel with rooms, where an apologetic owner explained that the water service was unreliable, but we could have a discount.

We refused the discount, stayed the night, then pushed on the next morning, passing huge groups of volunteers who were busy building shelters or distributing food. This worst of instances had brought about the best in people, and I felt a little guilty that on the night of the quake I had feared looters.

During our tour of Chile, details of just how powerful the quake had been began to emerge. It had registered as 8.8 on the Richter scale at the epicenter, with a reading of 8 in Santiago. Its effects had been felt as far away as New Orleans, where measurements in a lake detected the vibrations. Concepcion had moved a staggering almost ten feet from where it used to be; Santiago ten inches. Even Buenos Aires, on the other side of the Andes, had shifted nearly two inches. South America's tail had wagged, making maps of the world suddenly off the mark. The quake had been so violent that even the length of the day had shortened by a fraction of a second. The only way I could conceptualize this was to think of a picnic blanket laid out with food, glasses, and drinks dragged ten inches without anything falling over. Yet much of the country was unaffected by the quake—apart from feeling the need to help. It seemed incredible that anything had stayed standing.

The Minke family and I carried on with our travels into regions that geography had spared from any damage. We attracted many stares along the way, which at first I imagined signified that we were the first tourists in weeks, but then I suspected that we looked like a lesson in genetics. Papa Minke is a slim but commanding six feet, three inches; Mama Minke a statuesque five feet, eleven inches; and the Minke herself fits evenly between at six feet, one inch. My five feet, nine inches presumably made me look like their pet koala.

It was my second time to some of these regions, but I was able to look at them with fresh, if not quite high-set, eyes. Chile was not what I'd expected from South America—it has no jungles and is dominated by the Andean Mountains that give it its toothpick shape, but that wasn't it. Things functioned at a developed-world standard in Chile, and that had bothered me. I left Australia because I wanted to think on my feet and on occasion be afraid, all in the hope of feeling alive. In the aftermath of the quake, I felt selfish to begrudge Chile its advancement.

But the most important lesson had come the very morning of the quake, as we sat eating toast made over a gas stove while we waited for the power to come back on. Without Chile's development, things might have turned out very differently. Lisa, Harris, and Marguerite were as close to family as I could have without sharing DNA, and seeing them safe and unharmed made me very, very glad.

Fuerza, Chile.

13

Getting High in Bolivia

My newfound faith in human nature was perhaps well timed, as I had to take two weeks in London to do some book promotion. Lisa went to the wine regions of Argentina, and we arranged to meet up in San Pedro de Atacama, a small town in the world's driest desert.

Sometimes the rigors of travel can reap great rewards, like the unexpected sight of a condor in the city. Other times travel is like testing your breath by getting someone to kick you in the nose. This was how I felt after getting off a flight from London that had come via Dallas to Santiago. I had little time to do anything other than wash off the travel sauce and brush my teeth before getting onto a bus scheduled for a twenty-three-hour trip to San Pedro.

I was glad to be wearing rumpled T-shirts and battered sneakers instead of well-ironed clothes, and perhaps this was the reason my eyes began to droop just as the bus lurched from the terminal. Soon I was drooling onto the headrest of the unfortunate passenger beside me.

A few times that night I awoke, slurped, apologized, then repeated, but on the whole I had a not entirely unpleasant evening, waking as sunbeams pierced chinks in the drawn curtains and as passengers shifted and queued for the loo at the back of the bus.

When I went to stand up, I found that I no longer had any workable joints in my legs. After more than forty-eight hours of sitting, my knees had apparently left me for a younger man and only unlocked with a noise like the grinding of the Scylla and Charybdis.

Outside the view had changed from Santiago's sculpted lawns and office blocks to true desert, a place where rain was so rare that a few drops falling could wash away roads and be deadly—deadly, that is, if anyone lived here.

Anyone apart from miners.

The road swept past occasional mining operations where the tailings were piled in pyramids that evoked their Inca ancestors and strange mineral colors swirled through the rock like ice-cream toppings.

Finally reaching San Pedro, I felt the tightening of a headache and short of breath. San Pedro sits at just under 8,000 feet above sea level, so the oxygen content is significantly lower than Santiago at a mere 1,500 feet. With protesting lungs I trawled the town for my hostel. The local maps seemed intent on baffling outsiders and led me past every possible place but the one I was looking for.

I was surprised that the Minke was not waiting for me at the hostel. She'd been booked on a bus coming from Argentina. When she finally arrived four hours later, accompanied by a clearly insane man on a bicycle, he insisted that the town was not safe. It was, he said, a combination of New York and Miami. ("Have you been to either?" I asked. "No," he replied.) He seemed to want to offer his services as a guide, or bodyguard, but I politely refused.

Lisa wanted to press on the next day into Bolivia. She had had a hellacious journey that had included a three-hour wait at the Argentinean border, but she was eager to keep moving. I was all for recuperation.

"You can rest when you're dead," she pointed out, and while it felt like that state might come sooner rather than later, I agreed to the plan.

So the next day, still tasting airline food between my teeth, we trudged to an office and booked a three-day trip to Bolivia. There would be six of us plus a driver in a Toyota Land Cruiser with at least a little tread on the tires and T. rex decals on the windshield. Our chariot would take us over the Andes into Bolivia, then across the world's largest salt flats to a town called Uyuni.

From San Pedro we climbed, climbed, and climbed some more. The dry landscape was punctuated by occasional bursts of mineral color and the even more unlikely sight of high-altitude springs covered with lurid green and red algae, speckled with the pink of feeding flamingos. Then, just as incompatible with the surrounds, a solitary shack emerged and beside it a brightly colored Bolivian flag snapped in the strong wind. We had cleared Chile's border back in the town, and all we had to do now was get past this checkpoint. There was just one problem: Lisa's national pride.

"What is this country?" the border guard asked in Spanish, looking at Lisa's visa application. She had written *Gales*, the Spanish translation for Wales. She explained that it was near England and was part of the United Kingdom, like Scotland.

"It is not a real country," the guard said. "You are English." He crossed out *Gales* before writing *Inglatera* beside it.

The history of colonial bastardy by the English was about to wreak another tragedy. Lisa straightened to her full and imposing height, and I started to fear we might just see the inside of a Bolivian jail before the day was out.

I grabbed her and said, "Choose your battles."

She glared at me.

"Of course, Wales is a real country. He just can't be expected to know that, what with Bolivia not playing rugby," I said.

She didn't look convinced.

"They don't have schools either," I added.

She laughed, and we were stamped in. In no time we were back in the vehicle, shivering.

The temperature had gone from pleasant and sun-soaked in San Pedro to a harsh, windswept chill now that we had hit 12,000 feet. As the vehicle climbed farther we passed larger lakes, pausing occasionally for small herds of vicunas that scattered at our approach, their daintiness in stark contrast to their more famous relative, the camel. The lakes themselves were so saturated with naturally occurring minerals that they ranged from red to green, with shades of blue and orange in between.

Despite how toxic they looked, each lake had a population of flamingos working the water, long-legged avocets with their upturned beaks, and many smaller birds that always took off before I could get close enough to identify them, probably alerted by my harsh panting. Every step felt like a marathon, and just climbing a rocky outcrop for a better view left me wasted and wrecked—condor bait, if there were any condors around. This was the most inhospitable place I had ever been to. Parts of this range had never recorded rain, and the temperatures ranged from scorching in the lowlands to breath-fogging cold by the lakes.

Our group was made up of Europeans, apart from myself and Julio, our driver, who was Bolivian. In addition to my Welsh girlfriend, there was a French girl, a softly spoken young German man with spiky dyed red hair, and a Polish couple. The Polish couple spoke no Spanish, but the woman had some comprehension of English, so that became the common language.

"Can you breathe?" I asked her as she stumbled up onto the rock beside me. All she did was pant in reply, waving at her mouth to indicate she couldn't speak. Not only had I not been at altitude for some time, I had never been anywhere near this height at all. Australia and Botswana, the countries I have spent the most time in, are both markedly flat; their highest peaks are mere pimples on the landscape.

There's a single-mindedness that comes with being a birdwatcher, that seemingly most passive of activities, and so when we reached our final destination for the day, the azure Lago Colorado, I was determined to skirt its banks for new species. Lago Colorado is one of the only places on the globe where three species of flamingo can be seen, as well as many high-altitude birds such as the Andean goose, Andean avocet, and gasping foolfinch. (One of these was clearly made up by someone suffering from a lack of oxygen.)

The flamingos were easy to find, as were several of the larger species of bird. It amazed me how diverse the bird life was—we had peaked here at 15,000 feet, a punishing altitude for anything with lungs, yet I easily saw twenty species of birds in a small area. The way many enthusiasts with an irrational fixation do, I convinced myself there would be more—many more—on the other side of the lake. So I stumbled along, ignoring the dizziness I felt and the weakness in my legs. A drab brown bird called a cinclodes lifted off in front of me, so plain that it could only delight the most hardened bird nerd, which is exactly what it did for me, encouraging me to carry on.

A natural spring fed the lake, and I soon found its outlet, which was lurid green with algae. I was thirsty, but I feared drinking from even this most pure of natural sources might turn me green, like a feeble Hulk.

I pushed on, ticking a few more species off my list. It then dawned on me how stupid I was being, a remarkable moment of clarity considering how foolishly I'd been behaving up to that point. I couldn't breathe and couldn't move fast, and a mere stroll had me close to collapse. I had to get back to the car.

I'm too old for this, I thought, returning to my new favorite negative refrain. I might not be too old for adventure, but I was certainly too old for such stupidity. Getting back seemed improbable; doing it before dark, impossible. The sky was turning the same shade as the flamingos, and there was no artificial light between me and the camp. This was not a place to spend the night and wait it out—the exposure could kill you. It would only take hours with a temperature this low; I wouldn't even have the energy to shiver.

I'd told Lisa that I was going for a walk, but had neglected to mention exactly where. How long would it be before they sent someone to look for me? Would they have flashlights? This was Bolivia, what I had expected South America to be most like— charming but chaotic and makeshift. There probably would be no rescue.

The lake edge had a gentle curve that I needed to follow back on an ill-defined trail following its arc. I decided to take a shortcut, but soon realized my error as I sank almost to my ankles in rich, sucking mud. I was torn between hurrying and getting as far as I could or conserving energy and moving at a less lung-busting pace. I must have looked like an arthritic tortoise, and I felt even more decrepit. Earlier I had found the lack of oxygen and its effects a novelty—not exactly pleasant, but a new experience and therefore worth savoring. Now it scared me. I felt like I was drowning on land.

One step, then another. I paused, leaned over, and rubbed my thighs. They ached like I'd just run a marathon. I started moving again, making it only a few paces before stopping once more, my breathing now rapid and harsh, like a horny elephant that has spotted a breeding herd.

In the distance I saw a light and realized it was the campsite. I stumbled into some more mud; my shoes had become leaden lumps. I shook my feet, one after the other, and though the effort winded me, I broke into a stumbling trot, gaining at least twelve paces before tripping and falling onto all fours.

After a few rounds of this, I considered shouting but doubted my voice would sound any louder than a strangled fart. My throat was raw from taking drags off the thin air. It was a ragged figure that finally stumbled into the communal room and collapsed onto the bed assigned for me.

"You okay?" Lisa asked me.

"No," I said, but before our conversation could go any further, it became apparent from some squeaks and creaks that the Polish couple, not at all mindful of being in a well-lit room with four other people, were engaged in some under the blanky hanky-panky. How anyone could have the energy for that, I certainly didn't know. I didn't even think I could laugh about it until a guffaw emerged from my throat. Soon Lisa and I clutched at each other as we tried to muffle our giggles.

■■

The next morning I looked at the far side of the lake and berated myself for being such a drama queen. The distance I had stumbled wasn't really that far. Then I took my first few paces of the morning and my legs went dead and my head pulsed with flares of pain behind each eye.

Mountains are not my thing, I decided. I can't ski—my legs drift apart as soon as I set off and simply will not reunite—I don't like the cold, and while flamingos are all very nice, I wanted the jungle, where being a bird-watcher might get me killed by something like a jaguar rather than asphyxiation (definitely more dignified). There'd be no more getting high for me.

14

Take Me to the River

There's an old saying in Africa that goes something like this: "You're a bloody idiot, Peter Allison." Like many old sayings there is much truth to it, which may explain why I became overly excited at the idea of spending five days floating down a tributary of the Amazon on tire tubes. We were in the office of a small tour company, and I hopped from foot to foot like a child with a full bladder, while Lisa, unsure as to whether the trip was a good idea, wavered. Our other option was to take a motorized canoe, and the same journey could be done in three days. By comparison that seemed incurably dull to me, and with wheedling and puppy eyes, I convinced Lisa to choose the tubes. Before she could change her mind, we signed up.

At the time, nobody else had been interested, but when we all assembled, there were six of us—a young English guy named Nick; an Israeli ("Call me David," he said. "Not Ishmael?" I joked. "No," he replied. "My name is Adair. But call me David."); an Italian woman named Alisa; a Dutch couple; and a Spaniard named Thema with a bald and mottled scalp, who was the only person visibly older than me.

"Okay folks, here is the deal," said the man from the touring company, who spoke remarkably good English. "We cannot get through the blockade." Truck drivers, unhappy with some government figure, had blocked several routes out of La Paz and beat up any drivers who tried to get through. They were apparently tolerant of foreigners and might let them pass, but the situation could be inflamed at any moment.

My heart sank. Lisa's enthusiasm for the trip had grown, and she seemed just as crestfallen.

We were offered an alternative—an extra day for which we wouldn't be charged, and a mere seven-hour drive to an alternate launching point.

"The vehicle is not the most comfortable," admitted the man from the office. We all agreed to go.

The guide's name was Cesar (pronounced CHA-zar), and he was a deep-voiced man with the weathered features of someone who'd lived most of his life outdoors.

"And this," Cesar intoned in his bass rumble, "is our driver, Jesus."

Holy Roman Empire, I thought.

Jesus turned out to be a taciturn man with a ready bag of coca leaves stashed beside him. Coca is perfectly legal in Bolivia, and more people than not seem to have wads of it in their cheeks at any given time for the mild buzz it provides, and for its supposed benefits of increased concentration and alertness, as well as the alleged ability to combat altitude sickness. (Personally I found it made my mouth taste of leaves and did little else, except make my gums a little numb, which caused me to spill even more of whatever I was drinking than usual.)

With the driver and the guide, we were eleven people in a vehicle built for seven. Everyone agreed that Lisa should get the front seat with its greater legroom, as she was clearly the tallest of our group. I was scrunched in the narrowest seat at the back with the Dutch couple, a friendly pair who had the blemish-free skin of people who lived healthily and rarely saw the sun.

In front of me in a tight knot sat the four singletons, and we all chatted merrily as Jesus set off through the choked roads of La Paz. A wheel well that pressed into my buttock rendered my right leg numb almost immediately, but seven hours would be fine, I was sure. I would just need to shift around as if breaking wind on occasion to let blood reach my foot.

We soon left the winding mountain roads and hit the broad, open altiplano. These high-altitude plains have been agricultural stalwarts since the Incas and are still tended by poncho-wearing Quicha people, accompanied by desultory looking llamas.

Whenever we got to the flat plains, Jesus would put his foot down, while chewing monotonously on his coca. Our momentum abruptly decreased with a sudden bang, and the vehicle started to lurch. I felt a clawed hand clutch my thigh—I thought it belonged to one of the Dutch, then realized it was my own. We veered off the road, coming to a skidding halt some feet from the tarmac.

I'd changed countless tires as a guide, so I offered to help, just to give my shaking hands something to do. My offer was rejected and instead I threw one arm around Lisa, who I feared might be regretting coming on this trip with me. Jesus and Cesar got to work changing the tire, and we walked to the town ahead, where they would join us for lunch.

The air was chilly, but we were all keen for a decramping walk and the views were so spectacular, nobody much noticed the cold. We were in an elevated valley, and from the dead, flat altiplano, the

Andes loomed on each side of us, rising to impossibly high snow-capped peaks.

After only a few minutes, we were sprayed with dust as Jesus skidded in front of our strolling group and urged us back in. As soon as we finished our bland lunch of maize soup and a meat probably best left unidentified at a local cafe, we were on the road again.

We'd been driving for about three hours, and my back was already jarred from the uneven road and my right leg felt detachable, so I was comforted by the thought that we were close to half-way through the journey. So when Cesar said, without preamble, that the journey might take ten hours, we were all moved to a numb silence, broken only when, for no discernible reason, Thema started singing a few lines of a Spanish song in a deep but off-key voice before muttering something unintelligible.

To pass the time I started a sweepstake in the car. The estimates of our arrival time ranged from the cheery Dutch couple's optimistic seven in the evening (nine hours) to my cynical one in the morning (fifteen hours).

As it turned out, we were all optimists, and getting through the night would be one of the most frightening experiences I'd ever had.

■ ■

We left the altiplano in midafternoon and were on pure mountain roads again, a mix of dry dirt and gravel that pinged and ricocheted from the bottom of the vehicle, the dust permeating through the car's leaky seals and forming a paste in our mouths. We rarely saw other cars. Trucks were much more common than smaller vehicles, and they would fly past us on the narrow roads at suicidal speeds, rocking our car on its springs with a blast of wind and a toot of the horn, then enveloping us in blinding dust. And Jesus wouldn't even slow down when he was unable to see through the dust; he just drove on at the same pace until we emerged from the other side, miraculously always still on the road and not flying off one of the sheer cliffs.

"*Murciealago* . . . what is *murciealago* in English?" Cesar muttered at some point from the front, but his voice was so deep it carried all the way to the back.

While my Spanish was still far from fluent, one of the first things I learn in any language are animal names, so I was able to reply, "Bat."

"Yes! Bat! Who wants to see a bat?" Cesar rumbled, though not unpleasantly.

The other passengers and I all looked at each other blankly. Though the idea of a break from the cramped interior was appealing, I was also keen to reach our destination within a reasonable time. When I voiced my dilemma, everyone muttered, which left us nowhere. We needed a leader.

"I need to stretch my legs," Lisa said, and so it was decided.

After traveling down what felt like a goat track, Jesus stopped near the entrance to a cave, where for a paltry sum we were shown some stalagmites, stalactites, and bats that looked at us with an indifference that possibly mirrored our own.

"Nobody knows where this water goes," Cesar said, gesturing toward a good-size body of water covering much of the cave's base. "And there are legends that the Incas used to throw golden idols in here, along with human sacrifices, to please the gods.

Lots of people have looked for the gold, and some have wanted to explore to see where the water goes. The last group to do so were Japanese. None of them came back."

We squeezed back into our chariot. After heading back up the goat track, we rejoined the main road, but the two met at a ridiculously sharp angle. Any sensible driver would have looked for a spot wide enough to do a three-point turn.

Jesus didn't.

With a harsh yank of the wheel and no discernible change in the rate of his cud chewing, Jesus backed up toward the ledge.

I have two default settings when I'm scared, each one aimed at distracting myself from whatever it is that frightens me. One is to make grunting sounds like some aroused baboon, and the other is to be sarcastic. This time I reverted to sarcasm.

"Oh goody, Jesus thinks he can drive on air," I said.

The Dutch girl looked at me with crazed eyes, wondering how I could be flippant at such a moment.

This would be no three-point turn. Oh no, this was going to take several tries, and each one was making my internal organs squirm. Finally we got to a point where we were exactly ninety degrees to the road. Heart thudding, I prayed a truck wouldn't come and smash us straight off the ledge—if Jesus's driving didn't get us there first.

He reversed again, taking the rear wheels right to the lip of the ledge. Everyone remained silent, except Nicholas (the Dutch guy), who gave a strangled groan. I didn't want to look out the window, but my neck moved of its own accord. Through the narrow aperture that was the rearmost window I could see down—straight down. We were over nothing but air, and I damn near soiled myself.

"You okay back there?" Lisa asked, not turning around to do so.

"No," I squeaked.

I was sure the lip we were on was about to give way and that we would free-fall to excruciating death on the life-eating rocks below. I'm afraid of heights, but this irrational phobia was scarcely relevant to this extremely rational fear. For a brief moment I wished I was blind.

But Jesus revved the engine, and after several more scrotum-withering turns we zoomed away from the edge, the sound of the engine almost drowned by a collective exhalation.

■ ■

We'd been traveling for fourteen hours when we finally started to descend. The abject terror had returned because we were driving through utter darkness and fog so dense we couldn't see a foot in front of the car. A break in the darkness revealed several buses waiting out the fog, which suggested that what Jesus was doing (continuing to drive) was about as safe as juggling chainsaws or blow-drying your hair in a shark tank. Not even I would do that. Yet with Jesus at the wheel, we powered on.

Less than an hour passed before we burst from the fog into fetid and humid air, air that had oxygen in it, and a tang. It smelled of bananas, papaya, and other more exotic fruits and pricked sweat beads from our skin. The change was no less dramatic than waking up to find you'd turned into a kangaroo. Spontaneous conversation began around the car, jaws unclenched, fists unballed, and shoulders unhunched, and Thema sang a snatch of a song before breaking into his standard encore of muttered, unintelligible sentences.

Three hours later the euphoria of survival had worn off, and it was a grubby, grumbling bunch of travelers who disembarked from Jesus's jalopy in a bland little town somewhere between two places not marked on maps. The mussy-haired woman we'd woken up at the town's hostel was surprisingly chirpy. She showed Lisa and me and the Dutch to a Spartan room, cheerfully chasing out a cat.

Lisa and I had a much-needed hug, brief because we were both covered in sweat, dust, and road grime. "I just need the bathroom," she said. "Then bed, so I can straighten out."

Moving the unnecessary blanket on my bed aside, I found a chicken's egg on my sheets.

"Ah! *Huevo! Que bueno!*" (Ah! An egg! How good!") the hostel owner said in delight when I brought it to her, as if she'd won a prize.

Clearly the bed's previous occupant had been a chicken, and the sheets hadn't been changed since then, but I was too tired to care.

Lisa returned from the communal bathroom and advised us against using the men's (which shared a paper-thin wall with ours), unless it was of dire need.

I fell deeply asleep but was woken after what seemed like a very brief time by Cesar's bass voice shouting "*Vamos!*" ("We go!") before the rooster outside could crow.

After an extraordinary breakfast of steak, eggs, rice, lettuce, tomato, and instant coffee so dastardly that even my caffeine craving system rejected it, we were on the road again.

"Only three hours," said Cesar, smiling.

Sure.

It took another eight hours from breakfast to reach our destination, meaning that we'd spent over twenty-two hours stewing in our own juices in the four-wheel drive, not to mention enjoying near-death experiences and sheer terror. So it was a huge relief to be at the river for our relaxing float downriver. Little were we to know that this was where the real adventure would begin.

■ ■

Despite our delayed arrival, our raft wasn't yet ready for launch. The riverbank was strewn with litter from a nearby village and land mined with dog turds. While the setting was less than idyllic, the river looked inviting, but first we needed to meet our crew.

A hardworking man with a gold-toothed smile was lashing together tire tubes to a rectangular frame made of bamboo.

"Hmm, rubber, twine, and bamboo, not noted ship-building materials," I mused, watching him, though I quite liked the rough look of our vessel as it came together. Despite a near drowning the last time I was on a similar vessel, on the Sand River in South Africa, I had only one thought—how could this not be fun?

The gold-toothed man introduced himself as Abel and told us his wife, Reina, would be our cook.

"*Mucho gusto,* Reina," we all replied. Thema rolled the *r* at the front of her name as if he found it delicious.

One additional crew member sat watching us toadlike through heavy-lidded eyes. Though it was clear he put a lot of effort in at the gym, he didn't replicate it in the boat-building endeavor.

"Our son," Abel explained, a hint of resignation in his tone. He offered no name to us, and a few of us quietly agreed to think of him as "Captain Useless."

We boarded the boat, our luggage wrapped in two-ply-thick plastic bags. These doubled as our seats, and I quickly realized my bird book had nasty edges to sit on, and I resolved to pack it more sensibly the next day.

We set off into a side channel as the sun sank, our goal a much more impressive looking river only a few hundred feet away. We bucked a little where the waters met, but Abel's efforts with a paddle soon had us in calmer waters. Before long a feeling of absolute serenity overtook us. Jesus was no longer with us, and that was surely a blessing. Everyone was silent, enjoying the peace, except Thema, who started singing a few notes of some song, muttered, and then went silent again.

"We will camp in an hour," Cesar said, and we all burst out laughing at his sense of time. Though he probably didn't know what we were laughing about, he joined in, and for the next two hours we happily let the current take us into the night until we beached at an unnamed point in a remote part of the world.

"This feels like South America, doesn't it?" I said to Lisa.

"Yes, it does," she said, letting go of a tent pole quickly to squeeze my hand. "But I'll admit I can't see anything here so we might as well be in London."

■ ■

The next dawn, the camp we had set up in the dark revealed itself to be a flat mix of sand and river rocks (actually some of the rocks had made themselves known to my spine during the night). The river here was the color and opacity of milky coffee. On the opposite bank, about 150 feet away, men were already dredging and panning. In response to our questioning looks, Cesar explained they were miners looking for gold.

The miners set up a pump that emitted a dull thrumming, its outlet pipe spewing muddy waste straight back into the river, which explained the river's murky color.

As we set off in the boat again, I felt content. The river was serene, even though the jungle on either side was disturbed by human activity and the water often cloudy. The brochure hadn't mentioned that the herons, kingfishers, caimans, and otters I'd hoped to see would be absent—there was no way they could hunt in this murk— yet the peacefulness made it impossible to be discontented.

"I think we should all sing a song from our country," Thema interjected.

The silence that followed would have been awkward if we hadn't all laughed.

"No thanks," I replied. "I really don't know any, and even if I did, my voice is like a seagull's fart."

Thema seemed disappointed, and reversing his usual order, muttered a little, then sang, "Lahlahlah," and with some pact he had made to be irritating fulfilled, waited for us to fall silent so he could do it again.

"Cesar," I asked, "what is the name of this river?"

"It is the Rio Kaka," he replied.

It took a few moments for it to hit me.

"Shit Creek? That's fantastic!" I said, laughing, though nobody else seemed to share my delight in the waterway's name.

The day passed with little incident and few breaks. Cesar was clearly keen to make up the time lost by our late arrival by encouraging Abel and his loafing son to paddle while the rest of us sat, chatted, and tanned on the raft.

■ ■

We set up camp again in the dark, and the fire was lit first so Reina could make a surprisingly tasty meal, given her seemingly Spartan ingredients of plantains, bread, canned tuna, and a mystery sauce.

The next morning we were woken by what had become the familiar Cesar alarm clock. "Abel!" he would shout, and I could feel, not just hear, the rumble of his bass voice, "*Vamos!*"

On day three we saw fewer and fewer signs of people. The banks were no longer gouged by mining, and the river ran cleaner with more and more streams joining it from the surrounding low hills. Macaws flew overhead and branches shook with the weight of fleeing monkeys, a sign that they were most likely hunted in this area. Among the dense greenery were the occasional orchids, splashes of yellow or red tended by bees the size of birds, and birds the size of bees.

On the fourth morning we were woken by something far louder than Cesar's bass rumble. A harsh, sustained bellow—changing in pitch on occasion but never waning—began before sunrise and roused all but the dead from sleep.

"What the hell is that?" the Minke asked me.

"Howler monkeys. World's loudest land animal," I replied, grinning in the dark. I'd glimpsed them before in the Pantanal but hadn't heard them calling properly until now, and only knew what the sound was because there was simply nothing else it could be.

The aptly named howler monkeys kept their chorus going all through our breakfast, then went silent as they made off to find their own food. Despite a bit of sunburn and Thema's annoying outbursts just as I was dozing off, I was more relaxed than I had been in years. South America was teaching me that it wasn't just adventure I had given up to sit behind a desk. Feelings of peace were so foreign to me that at first I resisted them to avoid heartbreak once they evaporated. But the river won, and by the fourth day I was a little more animated than a carrot but surely much happier. Having Lisa to share it with made it even more special, and she whispered in my ear one night that she was glad we came on the trip, and even more so that we'd been on the same bus in Patagonia.

■ ■

On the fifth day, however, everything changed. Somehow we had made up the lost time from our late start on the first day and Cesar promised that we would make it to our destination of Rurrenabaque by nightfall.

"Lah, lah, lah," Thema replied flatly to the news.

"Oh come on!" I protested. "That's not even a song!"

Despite the pleasure we had all taken in the trip, we now began fantasizing about a shower, a bed that didn't deflate during the night, a drink, and pizzas. Reina's cooking had relied more and more on fried plantain—the savory banana that is a staple in many South American countries but without condiments is as tasty as an old sponge.

The scenery, which had been subtly changing since our trip began, gave way dramatically for the first time to sheer cliffs soaring on either side of us, their sides worn smooth from years of the river's work. Finally the water was clearer, and at last I saw some herons standing on rounded ledges and staring intently at the river, waiting to spear any fish that ventured too close.

Just as suddenly we emerged from the canyon, and the river fanned out to the greatest width we had seen so far, perhaps 650 feet across. The currents and countercurrents this change set up made the surface a sequin-dazzle of ripples, and our little raft jolted as if being dragged over cobbles.

A sideways thrust suddenly caught us, and, despite hard paddling from Abel and some desultory stirs at the back from his son Captain Useless, the raft was dragged close to the bank. A visible current ran against the river's flow—causing a line as definite as lane markings on a highway—showing where the two currents rubbed against each other. The circular span of spinning water covered almost the whole width of the river, and there was no way to avoid it. Soon we were heading back upriver, then the current that trapped us pushed us against the rocks and shot us back in the direction of Rurrenabaque. Yet this was no cause for celebration, because we were heading toward far more turbulent water. My heart thumped as I realized we were about to be sucked into the dangerous-looking whirlpool ahead of us.

The front left corner of the raft dipped down as we hit the swirl, and the water rushed up and over Abel, then onto Lisa, me, and English Nick. Bucking and bobbing, the raft spun around in a sickening cycle. Despite being drenched, Abel kept his rowing strokes regular and strong. As we spun faster and deeper into the whirlpool, I clutched at my smaller backpack like it was my baby. My larger backpack could be sacrificed, but this one contained all my most treasured possessions—a camera, my binoculars, and bird books.

The whirlpool abruptly spat us out, soaking everyone at the back, then the raft was caught once more in the crosscurrent and we shot back toward La Paz. Again, Abel leaned hard into his strokes. Glancing back I saw Captain Useless dipping his paddle like he was stirring tea and didn't want it to slosh out of his cup.

The whirlpool had an inexorable pull, and after one lap past the wall, we were sucked straight back into the center, sinking deeper, the water coming up to my waist and grabbing me like maniacal hands, pulling and tugging.

"Hold on!" I shouted, as much to myself as anyone else, as we spun deeper into the chaos of foam and turgid water. The stoic Abel kept paddling, somehow not flung from the raft despite having no handhold.

A sudden savage lurch ripped the paddle from Abel's grasp and accelerated us into the spiral of water. I looked back at Abel's son, who was now also empty-handed. Perhaps he had thrown his paddle away for fear of having to use it.

"Without a paddle!" I shouted, laughing hysterically despite the danger we were in. The whole raft angled sideways now, leaning into the vortex, and while it was not some science-fiction waterspout with a huge cavity that could swallow us whole, I did imagine that when we hit its middle we'd all be sent flying, and in that sort of water even Lisa, with her championship swimming title, might not escape.

The rear of the raft dipped then touched the middle. We spun and somehow crested out of the turbulence and back into the mad looping current. We could try to paddle for the bank, using our arms and whatever tools we had, then hand over hand the raft until we were past the vortex, but Abel and Cesar gave no orders.

"A paddle!" the Dutchman shouted, and we turned to see it bob to the surface, tantalizingly close. "I'll get it," he added, making as if to dive in.

"No! You'll die!" shouted Lisa, causing his girlfriend to clasp a vice-like hand on his arm.

We had one loose tube attached to the raft by twine, which we'd used as a dinghy of sorts when someone wanted off the main vessel. Lisa offered to get into it and scull her way to the errant oar, but Abel had a better idea. He reeled the tube toward himself, then used it as a life buoy to snare the paddle and draw it in.

Though unavoidable, it seemed insane to be heading back into the whirlpool. Abel leaned deeper into his strokes, and those of us sitting on his side used our hands to stroke along with him. The sucking noise of the whirlpool grew, and we drew closer, angling in despite the grunts of the effort aboard. Then the front of the raft nudged its edge, but did not dip, and instead we sailed past, the circle broken, on the way to Rurrenabaque.

"My God, did we almost die then?" came the voice of someone from the back.

"Yep," I answered, still looking resolutely ahead, still holding the raft so tightly I was amazed it didn't pop. A pulse thrummed in my ear, and I knew I was grinning from a thrill similar to what I felt whenever I had encountered potentially dangerous wildlife. "Makes you feel alive though, doesn't it?"

"Loony," said Lisa to no one in particular, but pecked my cheek.

Oh yes, I thought, loony for sure, but alive. Alive!

Drunk with relief, we laughed through the last leg of the trip and cheered the sun on as it threatened to break Cesar's promise of arrival by sundown. When the town came into sight as the barest solar sliver hovered over the river's surface, we cheered again.

"Nicely done, Cesar, nicely done," I said, still buoyant in the adrenal afterglow and not even minding when, to celebrate our arrival, Thema burst into song.

15

Puff, the Magic Canoe

Our three-hour road trip from Rurrenabaque to the staging point for another boat trip turned out to be an additional rattling South American drive, but only after we had spent two days luxuriating with warmish showers and well-stocked bars.

"Are my teeth loose?" I asked Lisa as we departed yet another overcramped vehicle with a different group of travelers.

"What? Which ones?"

"All of them," I said, grinning, taking absurd delight in an experience that could rattle limbs from their sockets and teeth clean out of your skull.

Unlike the slight chance of seeing wildlife on the epic rafting trip, this river journey would offer hairier conditions with the added bonus of jaguar spotting.

■ ■

Despite being landlocked, Bolivia maintains a navy, a relic from days before they lost coastal access in a war with Chile. We watched and waited while a Bolivian official, spruced up in his uniform, made sure that the flotilla of canoes we'd be traveling in for the next stage of our journey were counted and ticked off. He did so with all the professionalism that fully loaded battleships probably required, frowning as he double counted every vessel.

Meanwhile, our Bolivian guide, who had introduced himself as Eric, stood watching with a broad smile that we were soon to realize was permanent.

Eventually there were only a few canoes waiting to depart. "All those ones," said Eric, waving toward the now near-empty river, "will go too fast, and make too much noise. We'll go slowly, and quietly, and see lots of animals!"

Oh, I like this, I thought. So with smiling Eric in the rear, Lisa and I and a small group of tourists set off in the last canoe, saluting the naval officer who just glared back at us, maybe imagining a vast ocean he might one day command, or perhaps just imagining laying his eyes on one.

Unlike the jungle we'd gotten used to seeing on our rafting trip, this time we were surrounded by sprawling pampas on each side of this river. Pampas areas are tropical, but with far more expanses of open grassland. And while they lack the kaleidoscopic biodiversity of the jungle, we were likely to see more animals because the open expanses of the pampas allow viewers to see that much farther, and animals that live there are more accustomed to being watched by humans and are thus less inclined to run away.

Occasional trees sprang from the plains, and in places the riverbanks were overrun with scrambled shrubs and lianas in which monkeys clambered. Often the monkeys would beg for fruit from people in the passing boats. This kind of behavior often results from bad tourism practices, and I was glad to see that grinning Eric didn't encourage such activities.

As Eric steered us around the river's wending course, giggling at the monkeys and occasionally pointing out the caimans sunning themselves on the bank, my hopes rose that this was the right sort of place to see a jaguar.

"Oh my goodness!" Eric exclaimed, the phrase amusing from someone for whom English was clearly a second or maybe even third language. "I've never seen that!"

I swiveled around. Nearby, a flicker of movement became a ripple, and I realized I was looking at a caiman that had caught a snake—but not just any snake. It was an anaconda as long as the caiman itself.

"Wow! Take some photos please. The other guides won't believe me!" said Eric, laughing, as if their doubt was the funniest thing imaginable. Given the fact that Eric had been guiding for more than three years, any first sight of something was special. I felt my luck curve take an upswing and wondered if maybe, just maybe, we might see something very special here. Something with spots.

Not long after our sighting of the anaconda-eating caiman, a certain smell began to tickle my nose, which I recognized as the distinctive odor of marijuana. Puttering around a corner we caught sight of another canoe, moving even more slowly than we were, with puffs of gray white smoke emanating from the back of it. These were not from the motor. Then and there I dubbed the boat *Puff, the Magic Canoe.*

The *Puff's* guide stood at the back, wearing a khaki camouflage shirt with torn off sleeves and a knife of ridiculous proportions hanging from his belt. I've never been to a wilderness area that didn't have guides like him, the sort that take the job not because they love animals or the outdoors, but because they think it makes them look tough and will impress girls. In the front of the *Puff* stood one of the tourists, heavily muscled with a military-looking crew cut.

In countries with tourism, inevitably the least popular tourists will often be those who visit in the greatest numbers. In some parts of Africa it is Americans who are often unloved; in Mozambique, South Africans are sometimes reviled; the Brits have a reputation that precedes them in southern Spain. The *Puff*'s group was clearly a group of Israelis—the dominant and most disliked tourists in Bolivia—and what they were doing wasn't helping matters.

I didn't care where they were from, or that they were smoking weed, or even that they were making more noise than is sensible in a wilderness area, but my hackles rose as soon as I saw the muscled tourist reach down into the canoe, come up with a stick, and throw it at a caiman that was sunning itself on the bank.

The caiman's armored skin could easily take such a blow from a stick barely more than a twig, but it didn't matter. My anger had grown to an icy rage by the time he reached for another stick. Mutters of "What a wanker" began to emanate from our canoe.

He'll run out of sticks, I thought, steam all but pumping out of my ears. And he did run out. But then the *Puff*'s guide did one of the worst things I'd ever seen a guide do: He pulled over so the tourist could gather more ammunition. Apoplectic by now, I was ready to dive into the water, overtake their canoe, haul in the muscled guy, and then . . . Well, I had no plan, but I'd think of something that would hurt him before he drowned me.

Lisa made soothing noises and restrained me.

Now Muscles started throwing sticks at anything in sight, including a heron that fortunately sidestepped the stick in the last fraction of a second. Birds not only lack the caiman's armor, but have bones light and hollow for flight, and even a small blow can break their limbs. If the bird had been hit, it probably would have died.

By now I hated not just the stick thrower, but the guide as well. "Why doesn't he stop him?" I asked Eric, just to say something and unclench my jaw.

For once Eric was not smiling and just said, "That guide is not a good one."

I was also furious with the *Puff*'s group. Surely there was someone aboard who knew that this was wrong. Maybe he was such an alpha male that the men were cowed, but one of the women could have humbled him. Yet none did; they just puffed away at their joints and laughed at every missile he threw.

Impotence is something men fear in all aspects of life, not just while horizontal, and this was the worst sort I could feel, because there was nothing I could do about something that mattered deeply to me.

Finally the *Puff* slowed and nudged into a bank near the campsite they would be using for their stay, a sign festooned with the word FLECHA, Spanish for "arrow."

As we puttered within range of the *Puff*, I stood up abruptly, causing a slight sway in the canoe that Eric was forced to correct, taking us a little closer to the alighting group.

"Hey! Digestive exit!" I shouted, or words that described such a thing in crude biological terms.

Not surprisingly, they all turned to look at me.

"No you! Genital skull!" I shouted, and I was paraphrasing once more, waggling an outstretched finger at the muscled man as I ranted at him

Muscles just stood there looking baffled at the frenzy-faced little white man shouting at him until it finally dawned on me that he wanted to know what he'd done to earn this diatribe. Eric sensibly had not slowed down or deviated from course. He clearly didn't want to be part of any intergroup brawl, so I was now swiveled at the waist shouting back at Muscles. I fished for a strong finish but could only come up with, "Don't throw sticks!" Then, after a brief pause, I added, "At animals!"

And then we were past them.

I sat down, feeling a tad foolish, yet shaking with the adrenaline that any sort of conflict brings. Loud applause followed like the sound of many birds taking flight, and I realized my group was clapping for me.

As the ice left my veins, I wondered what the tattoo I'd seen on Muscles's shoulder was, since it was likely we'd run into his group again over the next few days. Maybe he was a commando, I thought. Maybe even a ninja.

I was dead. I just didn't smell it yet.

16

One Hundred Ways to Bleed

We arrived at our camp that evening to discover it was a shared one, and among the group already there was David (aka Adair) from the rafting trip. After a quick catch-up, our conversation topic turned to the antics of his countrymen that afternoon, with the Minke describing the stick thrower's behavior.

David was very embarrassed. "He's probably right out of the military. They come here because it's cheap, but they're just looking to let off steam and probably have no real interest in where they are."

"Don't worry, one day I'll meet you in Bali, and then I can be embarrassed by Australians," I said.

I described the shape and positioning of Muscles's tattoo.

"Hmm, really?" said David. "Ex-commando."

"So not a ninja then. Thank goodness." I said.

"He's the sort of guy who knows a hundred ways to make you bleed."

"Excellent. Thanks," I said, wondering if I'd be seeing Muscles again in the near future.

"Pretty brutal what they do," said David. "Hopefully you won't run into him again.

"I'm sure I'll be fine," I said. And though I didn't really believe what I was saying, I still didn't want to regret what I'd done.

"Okay. Just be careful though. Those guys aren't known to be forgiving."

"Please feel free not to tell me any more."

Yet the conversation continued good-naturedly at the table that night and only increased my worry about some sort of ambush.

The mere thought of conflict usually made my eyes water. I'd long thought there was no finer form of self-defense than absence, and I had faith in my one athletic gift—my speed as a runner. But revelation came in the form of a quote from Winston Churchill, who once said, "I do not trust a man without enemies. It means he has never stood up for anything." I believed in the stance I had taken on the boat and did not mind having an enemy. I just wished it was one I was more likely to defeat in combat.

"I have a plan. I'm going to blame Aaron," I said to Lisa, pointing at the largest member of our group, a huskily built Australian who loomed over even her with broad shoulders and an imposing beard.

"Won't work," said Lisa. "The commando saw your mouth moving. And your hands flapping around."

"Aha!" I exclaimed. "I'll just have to say he's a ventriloquist and had his hand up my bum."

"You really have no shame, do you?" Lisa said, with more resignation than dismay.

We only had three days left on the tour, and I tried to convince myself that maybe we would not see the commando again, or if we did, I speculated, maybe he wouldn't be so bothered by the names I had called him, or perhaps he had rethought his actions and was now devoting his life to conservation. While I knew both those options to be as unlikely as peace in the Middle East, I had to have some hope. Secretly I wanted to carry on my tirade at him, in greater depth, but not without the safety of a machine gun, from some distance.

The very next day we saw their group trudging through a swampy section of the pampas in search of anacondas. Their guide, still in his macho vest, held one up above his head with a roar of triumph.

Before we'd set out, Eric had cautioned us against picking up any anacondas, not only because some of them were big enough to eat us, but also because it was impossible to know what sort of stress it caused them. Most of us were wearing insect repellent, which might harm them. At the sight of the snake being manhandled, the usually smiling Eric stormed over and gave a rapid-fire mouthful of invective to the other guide, who had draped the anaconda over one of his tourist's necks. Despite his unimpressive physique, Eric's tone had sufficient authority that the snake was quickly released and Macho's group moved on. Luckily the commando didn't see me standing behind Lisa.

■ ■

On the final day of our tour, without having had a whiff of jaguar, we set out before dawn to do some wildlife watching before the nocturnal animals (mostly predators) settled down for the day. Eric guided our canoe to a high bank of the river, and after scrambling up it we were rewarded with a view of the surrounding flatlands and the wobbling sun as it rose. It was so serene that I stopped thinking about the commando and how I had not seen a jaguar, and exhaled.

My reverie was soon broken by the revving of a motor, and another canoe came to what I already thought of territorially as our spot.

"Oh goody," I thought, seeing the distinct military haircut at the bow. At least he wasn't standing. At least he didn't have sticks. It surprised me that his group had managed such an early start, as they seemed more intent on partying rather than on finding wild-life, but they now moved with some urgency up the bank to catch the last of the sunrise—a futile measure, as close to the equator the sun ejects from the horizon like bread from a toaster.

As their group formed up, they maintained a distance from us in the way two herds often do when they meet. I kept my eyes firmly on the commando, ready to break eye contact (and probably wind) if he looked at me. He stood aggressively, shoulders bunched as if ready to swing his arms into violent action, the pose of an alpha gorilla unlikely to let an insult pass. Usually I aim to defuse tension with humor, but there would likely be a language barrier, so my only chance was to make a dive for the river and rely on the unlikely hope that commandos can't swim.

One member of the *Puff*'s group broke away and headed into some waist-high grass behind us. The movement made the commando look my way with a scowl. I turned around and braced myself to take a running dive.

From behind us came the rasp of a zip, clear in the still morning air. I waited for the gush of urine to follow (in impolite proximity to the gathering, I thought). Instead there was a girlish squeal, the thunder of feet, and a Hebrew curse that was effectively guttural.

Both of our groups had been facing the now-risen sun, watching its reflection redden the water, but now swiveled en masse at the disturbance. The erstwhile urinator had woken a sleeping capybara that was now desperate to escape being peed on—or was perhaps furious at the indignity of it all—and was doing what capybara do when threatened: heading for the water. Unfortunately our group was in its way.

Capybaras can weigh up to one hundred pounds, and this one was coming at us at ramming speed. It looked big enough to cause injury, and I really wished that I knew what to do. Stand my ground or run? Throw a commando at it and let them sort it out?

There was no time to decide. Several of us threw ourselves out of harm's way as the rodent charged through the gap we'd made. It then scampered down the bank and plunged into the river, and its splash exposed a jagged stump that would have impaled me had I made my diving exit.

Both groups re-formed like schooling fish, but this time with no gap between us. Most people were laughing, which is a common response to shock. I was chuckling away too, but warily eying the commando for a few tense seconds before Eric said it was too crowded and we should move on.

I waited for a voice to call me back or a sucker punch to the back of my head, but we returned to our canoe without incident. This made me wonder if the commando had considered his sins and felt some shame, or whether he was mellower than I had given him credit for, or dulled by dope.

All I knew was that even though I had stood up for something that mattered to me, diplomacy might be the better path in the future. I probably hadn't taught him anything; he probably respected my stand as much as a pigeon respects a statue. Nevertheless, I felt a little proud, even if it had taken a giant guinea pig to save me.

17

The Idiot Box

Over the years I've been approached four times by producers who'd read my books about safari guiding in Africa and were interested in making a TV show based on them. While these opportunities have always dried up, I received another call while I was traveling in South America. This one felt different, and I started getting excited.

Back in Australia the occasional day's test filming had led to adventures like being locked in a cage with white lions—a welcome escape from my office routine and a reminder of what I was passionate about. Though the concept of being on television caused me some mixed feelings, since I cherish the relative anonymity of publishing books without becoming physically recognizable in public, there were some good reasons to be enthusiastic this time. The production company that had contacted me had agreed it was a priority of theirs to highlight issues of conservation. A show would also fulfill my desire to continue traveling the world watching animals and would pay far better than writing alone could.

Lisa and I were traveling farther north, and when the production company called again, we agreed that the best place to meet was Colombia. Lisa didn't care to accompany me for the test shoot. She went ahead alone to Cartagena, a colonial town on the Caribbean coast. I would join her three days hence.

"Is it really safe here?" the cameraman, named Michael, asked when I met him at the Bogota airport. He was referring to the country's reputation for being a hotbed of violent criminal activity run by drug lords.

"Seems so," I replied, which was true as far as I could tell.

The truth was there was *some* danger in our plan for the next two days. I'd arranged a naturalist guide to accompany us, but we were heading into more obscure parts of the country, and there might still be rebel activity in these areas. There was also a chance we'd encounter pumas, bears, snakes, vampire bats, and maybe, just maybe, a jaguar. Still, despite Michael's fears, I was eager to get out of the city and into the wild, though I would miss having my little whale as a sidekick.

The next day our guide, Diana, and our driver, Eduardo, met us at four in the morning. From the look of his shaved head and bulging muscles, Eduardo was likely to be fine at security too. His vehicle was tiny, its wheels not larger than dinner plates. He drove with an arm out the window by necessity as much as fashion.

Bogota is the world's second-highest capital city (after La Paz in Bolivia), but Eduardo drove us up higher still. We passed panting cyclists struggling in the thin air, and I found the mere idea of exertion in this oxygen-depleted part of the world tiring.

After several hours' drive, and a pause to partake of a local energy brew consisting of hot water, huge chunks of palm sugar, and a slab of rubbery white cheese, we reached Chingaza National

Park, open only by special permission. The power a camera can wield became evident as the guards checking our papers were more interested whether we were famous than if anything was out of order.

After completing the security formalities, we moved immediately into a place of clear streams, tussock grasses, as well as alien-looking plants with hairy leaves on dead-straight stems. Everything glistened with dew and our breath fogged with each exhalation. This habitat, called paramo, consisted of high-altitude wetland that was home to strange species such as the mountain tapir, as well as more cosmopolitan animals like pumas and the continent-spanning white-tailed deer.

"More energy!" Michael shouted as I was doing my first piece for the camera.

Whenever animals are the subject of general conversation, I become very animated and tend to flap my jaw at the person I'm talking to until their ears bleed. But in front of a camera is a different thing, and I found it hard to muster anything more than a dry monotone while addressing the lidless eye of the lens and its slow blinking red light.

"Paramo," I said blandly, "is high. Cold. Wet."

"More energy!" Michael called again, making me think of all the wildlife television hosts I'd seen in recent years who hop like mountain goats from place to place, going into rapture at any critter they encounter.

To show that I wasn't beyond such lunacy myself, I got the idea of sampling a plant, unwise in an area where my knowledge of botany was less than thorough. Maybe some plant compound could give me the manic juicing I needed to cut it on film. I spied something that looked a little like rosemary. As I spat out the bitter pith Michael said, "Great! Let's get some more of that sort of stuff!"

We spent most of the day checking likely habitats for pumas. Michael encouraged me to make as much noise and gesticulate as wildly as possible for the camera, so loudly that any sensible cat would flee in protest.

"Look at this!" I shouted, gesturing at a pile of bones I'd found after I climbed onto a small ledge.

Michael followed, slipping and sliding on the mossy rocks as he continued filming. Michael was so out of his element in the wilderness that he made me feel like a ballerina. Gasping for breath, he eventually made it to the ledge.

"Puma kill!" I said, genuinely excited now. Attached to the bones were some withered strips of sinew, skin that was turning to leather, and a foot. "See this! Not a hoof . . . looks like it was a fox!" I was happily playing wildlife detective as I looked around the carcass surrounds and located the distinct pug marks of a puma, still fresh in my mind from my days with Roy. "Yes! Definitely a puma kill—not so fresh, maybe even a week or more, but the overhang has protected the tracks from rain. Nice!"

"Hey," Michael said, "that was excellent. But you can hear my breathing on the tape. Can you do it again, with the same amount of energy?"

■■

Over dinner that night Michael revealed that this was his first wildlife shoot—he normally worked in a studio. It turned out he had shot several feature films I'd seen and enjoyed. Movies are a side passion of mine, and we stayed up talking about his work later than we should have, given we'd scheduled another brutally early start for the next day.

When I expressed concern at being tired the next day, Michael assured me that if I could be as animated as I'd just been we'd be able to nail it.

Nail it, I did not.

With no emotional feedback from the lens I came across as cold and emotionless as a toilet bowl, but nowhere near as deep. On day two we traveled to the lowlands, a place of tangled trees and busy streams, chattering with birds and monkeys. There might be jaguars here, but Michael, keen to get a worthy performance from me, kept calling for more energy, and by energy he meant noisy enthusiasm. If all the ruckus I made didn't drive away the wildlife, then the strange rictus I wore to show my keenness just might. Watching the playback, I saw someone who looked like me but with a leery grin that would make sensible people lock up their daughters.

Michael took long shots of me seeing patches of the jungle for the first time that captured my genuine passion for all wild places, but the interspersed close-ups spoiled any useful footage he had.

Michael planned to shoot the last segment in a cave, which excited me because it held five species of bats, including the type with long fangs that drink blood; in other words, vampire bats. Bats that sucked blood were a lot more interesting than my last encounter with the creatures, and I was keen for a close look.

"Don't forget, you need to project lots of energy!" said Michael as we headed into the cave. Already that day I had climbed trees and a rock face to demonstrate that I was not a zombie, and while I did appreciate the opportunity being offered to me, suddenly the whole idea of appearing on screen was wearisome.

Yet real energy came to me when I met my first vampire bat. I'd read up on them in anticipation of this trip and knew they were unlikely to be dangerous—less than ½ percent of bats carry rabies. (In fact non-bloodsucking bats are more dangerous because their dung can harbor a fungus that causes a deadly lung disease.) Rising to my full height in the cave, I came eye to eye with a roosting vampire and gave it a genuine smile. My teeth are one of my more prominent features, and smiling at animals is generally a bad thing, because animals take it to mean you are about to bite them. I was too happy though to bear that in mind. All the other bat species in the cave took off before I could get this close, but the vampires all flashed their fangs straight back at my unintentional threat. Unlike other bats, vampires are able to run on the ground, an adaptation for their bloodsucking lifestyle. Usually they locate warm-blooded prey, such as a cow or even a sleeping human, land nearby, then walk on their back legs and elbows before making incisions with their razor-sharp teeth and lapping at the flow of blood that results. While doing this their saliva mingles with the blood, releasing an enzyme with the truly wonderful name of Draculin. This stops the blood from clotting, so the wound leaks well after the bat has had its tablespoon or so of dinner.

I knew all this, but I didn't know that vampires can also run while upside down, so when one scurried along the cave roof toward my face, I was taken aback.

"Hey!" I said sharply, as if dealing with a cantankerous lion (and forgetting that this bat probably only understood Spanish).

I'd always been taught not to run away from large animals, and had held my ground against lions, elephants, leopards, and the like. But as I took a step back from the bat, the stones clattered under my heels. The sound I'd made disturbed the other bats in the cave. Several thousand pairs of wings beat the air, though not one bat touched me during the maelstrom, so adept are they at using sonar to avoid obstacles.

Michael gave a not-so-manly squeal as one of the vampires dive-bombed him, flying straight at the lens. Later he showed me the playback, and the widescreen he was using certainly made the bat seem more threatening, but his undignified exit from the cave had me quite amused. He was okay, so I suggested we get back to work while I was still showing signs of life.

I as reentered the cave, I heard Michael stumbling behind me. It is difficult to look through a camera and cover uneven terrain simultaneously. When I heard him say, "More energy—but move slowly!" I burst out laughing. One of the remaining vampire bats devised a fitting punishment and relieved himself copiously onto my shirt.

"Oh man, that stinks!" Michael said.

"I'm just glad it wasn't Robert Pattison," I replied.

"Hey man, that's funny. Say it again!" Michael said, swinging the camera toward me.

Unfortunately on the second take my delivery was flat.

■ ■

E-mails between me and the company trickled to a stop in the few months after this performance. I was not offended and knew much of the blame lay with me. I had known it was a long shot anyway, but I felt some small disappointment—it could have been a dream job, to get paid well to travel and be with animals and teach people about conservation. But at the same time, I was glad I failed. At last I'd found a field where I just wasn't a big enough idiot.

18

Beekeeping in the Amazon

"Honey, what did he say?" the woman asked her husband, even though the man she hadn't heard was standing right by her, could hear her, and understood English.

"He said it was to the left of the tree," was her husband's answer, not a helpful one as we were in the rain forest and trees were pretty plentiful.

"Oh," she said, apparently satisfied. Then, mouth agape, she pressed binoculars to her face and began a hectic scan—up, down, left, right, and back—but the bird she was trying to see evaded her.

"Darn it, where has it gone?" she asked, though the bird hadn't moved.

"To the left of the tree," I replied mischievously, able to do so because I wasn't guiding this group. I hadn't been a guide for ten years.

A man named Oscar was in charge of our group, and he'd been in the guide business for twenty years straight. The down-turned lines set firmly into his face suggested he only smiled when paid to do so. I felt for him. There was nothing monumentally wrong with this group. They weren't unpleasant. They weren't overly demanding. They were just really irritating.

Maybe I was prone to irritation because after eight months of traveling mostly with me, Lisa had headed back to London, her time for travel used up. "Don't do anything I wouldn't do!" she shouted to me as she boarded the plane. "Like pee standing up?" I replied, mock perplexed. The last sight I had of her was her shaking her head, and I wondered as I so often did why she liked me. I would not see her for two months until I visited her in the United Kingdom.

The troublesome tourists were a real problem for Oscar. He needed to make sure everyone enjoyed his or her stay at the beautiful Sacha Lodge, a property on the banks of the River Napo in the Ecuadorian Amazon. An island of jungle surrounded by oilfields and logging interests, this patch of forest depended on tourist dollars, so keeping people happy was not just Oscar's job but a deeply important responsibility.

This was the first time since arriving in South America that I had work to do, but what lovely work it was! The owners of the lodge had been on safari in Africa and were impressed by African guiding standards. They'd asked if I would spend a month at Sacha and let them know what they could do better. I was grateful to be doing this, because the property was not only beautiful but fascinating, aswarm with different species of monkey, more birds than the whole of Southern Africa, and two amazing structures that allowed you to climb above the forest canopy and look for the species that rarely descended, such as sloths or howler monkeys.

Of course my role as spy was not entirely comfortable. All the guides knew I'd worked as a guide, but none of them knew I was on a mission from the boss. The guides I'd been out with were all very impressive and professional, so all I felt I could do was offer a big endorsement and an apology for not being able to help more than that.

"I realized today that working with tourists is like working with bees," I said later to Dan, one of the guides who'd shown me around before I joined Oscar's group.

"How so?" he asked, looking through a book of the region's snakes to try to identify a species he'd seen earlier that day.

"Most days are fine, you enjoy your job, maybe even love it," I began, "but then one day you get a prick. You can handle these, but over time, the pricks accumulate, until finally your system can't take it anymore, and one day you are allergic. And once you are allergic, you can never work with bees again."

"Okay," said Dan, unimpressed by my analogy.

I wandered off, pondering my bee sting epiphany.

Being irritated by the people in his group was not just a problem for Oscar, it was upsetting me too, because I was well aware my traveling days would eventually come to an end, and at some point I'd need to start making money. But I simply could not return to Sydney and plug away at a job I cared nothing for in the hope that I would get ahead in life.

TV was out. But while I wasn't a big enough idiot for TV and was probably too idiotic for a desk job, I had in the past been precisely idiotic enough for guiding. Sharing my passion for animals and the wilderness was perhaps the only work I was ever good at. Before even arriving in Sacha, I'd thought that maybe, just maybe, I would fall in love with the place and be invited to come out of my long retirement from guiding and take a job there.

But Oscar's group made me think I was still allergic to tourists. It didn't have anything to do with Oscar, who was a great guide with sharp eyes and an encyclopedic knowledge of bird calls. We ticked off species with the sorts of names that make non-bird-watchers roll their eyes—rufous-capped ant thrush, white-browed wood wren, short-billed foliage gleaner, and the quite lovely blue-crowned motmot. But the woman who kept insisting she couldn't see, or hear, what we were looking at was really irritating. It occurred to me that she might be partially deaf, or blind, and I felt like a thorough bastard for holding her in disdain. Then her husband spoke to her in a low whisper and she understood him perfectly, so I went back to being irritated.

Perhaps my intolerance was fed by my own uncertainties about things, too. I hadn't spotted a jaguar yet, and while the cats might occasionally pass through Sacha, none of the guides there had ever seen one on the property. The closest I'd come was some tracks of a big cat Dan had told me about that tourists had trampled over before I could look at them. But in all honesty it wasn't the jaguar I was missing, really. It was more that I hadn't found a life. I'd hoped that South America would inspire me in the same way Africa had and that I could settle in for a while before the urge to move on overtook me again. So far, however, there'd always been a reason to move on—and not enough to stay. I'd follow Lisa almost anywhere, but not to London, where she lived for years at a time before she would scratch her itchy feet and travel again. London would deaden me as surely as Sydney, and she understood this. Homelessness didn't bother me, but I needed to find some way to make a living.

My musings were interrupted by Oscar. "Look! Leftie the light!" he said, gesturing excitedly with his laser pointer. I spun around, just in time to see a monkey pop into view. It was about the size of a house cat and entirely black except for a cute white patch around its mouth and nose that explains its Spanish name (*beber leche*—"drink milk"). More monkeys followed, and soon the whole troop was crossing overhead, using branches as trampolines.

"Wow! Monkeys!" the woman exclaimed loudly and stood there slack jawed, head back, watching their passage. Only then did I realize that she hadn't noticed them until that point. Her voluminous call proved too much for one monkey, and his bowels loosened in fright.

If there was a god as vindictive as I was, the mess might have landed in the woman's mouth, but instead it splattered her backpack. And despite the immediate rotten fruit aroma, she didn't notice this either—or my mirth.

"Nice shot, monkey," I whispered, admiring its aim as much as I had its earlier gymnastics. However juvenile my pleasure, I was brimming with happiness, and I shed my earlier worries. This was not Africa, I had to remember, and to compare it to Africa was as foolish as measuring it against Paris. And to dislike this woman just for her rudeness to guides and general blandness reflected far more poorly on me than it did on her. Perhaps my disdain was rooted in fear—that I might become like her if I couldn't find a worthy way to spend my life. It was time to take all the joy I could from South America and live and laugh as much as was possible in the extraordinary places I visited.

And yet, my inner devil said, *It would have been great if it landed in her mouth, right?*

19

All You Can Eat

There was much to like about life as I lazed between activities at Sacha Lodge. I was seeing animals, coming across new species of all kinds from anteaters to electric eels, and eating bounteously. In fact walking the trails had no counter effect to the amount I was eating, so I decided I should take advantage of the lagoon in front of the lodge and get some exercise more strenuous than mastication.

Shaped like a bowl, the lagoon stretched perhaps 3,000 feet on either side of the lodge's deck, its dark waters meeting the shore roughly 650 feet opposite. The far bank was cut occasionally by channels that drained the surrounding swamps and gave the lagoon its dark tea color. A short grassy section gave way to tall trees alive with monkeys and birds.

At the first sight of the lodge, I'd been surprised at its position by the lagoon, thinking it would be heaven for mosquitoes but hell for anyone with blood in his or her veins and skin to be punctured. However, the water from the swamps was rich in tannins leeched from decaying leaves and too acidic for mosquitoes to lay their eggs in. As a result, the deck overlooking the lagoon was unspoiled.

One day I was standing on said deck eyeing the diving board mounted at its edge. Raised a mere six and a half feet from the water's surface, it was still enough to spur on my fear of heights, and I started making excuses to myself not to use it, only to be answered by the voice of rationality. What if a stump was hidden underneath the water? (They had all been cleared long ago, doofus.) What if an enormous caiman had just moved in? (No enormous caimans have been seen for years, wimp.) What if I landed straight on an electric eel? (Eels are nocturnal. Be a man and get on that board!)

That rational voice was a bastard but had irrefutable arguments, so I took a few swift steps up the ladder to the board and launched off its end, my body arched, my hands held out in front like my swimming teacher had taught me many years before, breaking the surface tension with my fingers before the rest of me plunged through. My swimming teacher perhaps would have been satisfied, but I was not at all delighted when my testicles somehow got slapped hard enough that I felt them in my throat.

Clearly I should have worried less about animals in the lagoon and concentrated more on my own poor form. Usually I have a slothful attitude toward exercise, and therefore the physique to match, but with a full month ahead at Sacha, it was my best chance to regain some of the fitness I'd lost since leaving Roy.

After recovering from the dive, I committed myself to taking advantage of the lagoon and going for a swim each day. I planned on building slowly, until I went to the other side and back. Not so great a challenge, but on my first attempt I wasn't even halfway when I felt my legs lagging and my head sinking lower with each stroke. I was doing the breaststroke, and the monkeys that watched from the far shore dipped their heads up and down in mimicry of my bobbing dome.

Deciding that I preferred obvious failure to the embarrassment of needing rescue, I swam back to the swimming platform just as one of the guides, a perpetually upbeat chap named Gustavo, began setting up rods for his guests to go piranha fishing.

"Are you crazy?" one of them shouted at me with an American accent.

"Nah, Australian," I replied.

I wasn't sure how wise it was to be in the water at the same time as their bait—chunks of chicken that the piranha were experts at nibbling off the hook without ever hitting the metal—but I remained unmolested as I hauled myself out.

The next day I was determined to make it at least halfway across the lagoon before turning back. I steeled myself to overcome the lack of resolve with respect to exercise that has plagued me my whole life.

"Oh dear," I thought as I launched off the board, arching my back sharply like a cocked eyebrow to avoid the indignity I'd suffered the day before. I had spied the head of an aged man visiting the lodge on the other side of the lagoon by the grassy patch. He had evidently made it to the other side. There was no way now I could only go halfway. Being ruled by testosterone is a pain in the ass sometimes.

I began my slow breaststroke, feeling fatigue almost immediately as my muscles complained. Relief followed as they warmed and stopped their whining momentarily. There was some joy as I got farther than the previous day's capitulation point—then weary leadenness set in as the exertion started taking its toll.

The old man gave me a merry "Ciao!" as he swam by. My reply was a gasped "Hoo!"—the only sound I could manage.

I made it to the other side, trod water a while, then steeled myself to head back. The deck looked ridiculously far away as I set off, a moon landing of a swim. As I splashed and paddled, I distracted myself by watching the birds around the lagoon's edge. Doves cooed. Hoatzins clapped their wings as they made the most inelegant flight of any bird. Kingfishers dipped into the water for prey then beat their catch against branches before swallowing it. And from somewhere unseen came the maniacal, funky-beated, and outrageous call of a wood rail.

Gustavo was with new guests when I got back. Shooting me an amused look as I hauled myself out, he said to his group, "I recommend swimming to you all, you can see it is safe, but maybe don't go across to the other side. Just stay around the platform." I wondered if there was something I'd missed on my list of potential diving board disasters.

■■

Within days I was doing the swim across the lagoon with relative ease and was planning on building up to two laps. My only fear was of caimans. Two different species of caiman lived in the lagoon, the inoffensive spectacled caiman, never a problem even when it reached its maximum length of six and a half feet, and the black caiman, a confirmed man-eater in some parts of South America, and the largest of its family.

"There's a large black caiman in there," Gus told me one day.

"Huge?" I asked, echoing Marcello from the Pantanal.

"Not huge. Just large. Maybe nearly ten feet. But it usually stays over the other side of the lagoon, near that channel the canoes use to bring guests in."

Usually is not a comforting word when applied to wildlife, as animals are as changeable as the weather. *Ten feet* was even less comforting, as a caiman that size would be more than capable of dragging me down, pulling me apart, and snacking on me as needed while my bits decomposed. (I think about crocodilians a lot, so know the process through every grim step.)

"Even the one under the deck could get upset if she thought you were going for her babies, even though she is a spectacled."

"How big is she?"

"About six and a half feet."

This length wasn't that comforting either. I'd known about the caiman under the deck, but I had yet to see it and had not realized it was quite so large. Suddenly the diving board seemed the least of my challenges as I tried to gather back the bravery that I'd lost at my desk job.

The night that I'd spoken with Gus, there was a barbecue dinner on the very deck I swam from each day. Meat sizzled and delicious aromas drifted through the jungle, making many stomachs gurgle hungrily.

I joined a small cluster of tourists and a guide making their way to the deck, when a voice from under it called "Mom!" and I was transported back to Bolivia, and Parque Machia.

When the puma volunteers had walked toward the pumas' cages, they shouted out "Hola!" so the puma knew who was coming toward them. Roy usually answered with a hearty, snarling yowl. Sonko, Roy's chubby nemesis, squeaked out something that sounded like a cigarette-smoking, sea-urchin-gargling, baby American crying, "Mom! Mom! Mom!"

Hearing this sound coming from under the steps leading to the deck now, I knew it was not some lost child, but a baby caiman. They can be quite cute, so I stepped around the stairs for a closer look, off the platform and to the water's edge. Rookie error, that move.

"Mom!" came the sound again. But unlike Sonko, who was just saying hello, this baby caiman meant exactly what it said.

"Bugger," I thought, just as a wave started coming toward me. I jumped backward, then sideways, not because I was a nimble sidestepper but because it was the only way back onto the steps. One of the other tourists staggered away, sure I was about to be eaten; another gave a strangled croak; and the guide who had just stepped away came back and laughed, then shone his torch under the deck.

Mom was only about four feet long.

Probably not worth the reaction then.

Based on Gus's exaggeration of the deck caiman's size, I decided that the black caiman across the lagoon (who I had yet to see) was most likely not the alleged ten feet either.

■ ■

With renewed confidence, the next day's swim was a pleasure, and I started doing one and a half laps, feeling not a hint of nervousness. Apart from caiman, I felt a mild concern about candiru, a fish that makes you understand just how mean a streak evolution possesses. Small and narrow, like half a worm, it usually latches onto the gills of larger fish, lodging itself in with sharpened fins and feeding on the soft flesh inside—not pleasant for fish, but nothing compared to what it does to humans. Somehow it homes in on the smell of urine before it proceeds straight up the urinary tract in either gender. (While it's thoroughly nasty, it can't swim straight up a urinary stream of anyone foolish enough to pee into the river as sometimes reported.) Once inside the urinary tract, the candiru's barbed fins come out and it eats away, driving the host mad with pain—rumors abound of many a man performing an autopeotomy rather than live with it inside.

I had been told that candiru were not in the lagoon for the same reason mosquitoes were absent—it was too acidic. Nevertheless I was glad for the mesh insert in my swimming trunks that would act as an extra barrier to any tough-skinned candiru that might be around. I also, as a matter of course, did not pee in the lagoon.

So any concerns and local advice was seemingly baseless— but a powerful imagination turned out to be my undoing. One night a clump of vegetation broke away, or came in on a channel, forming a floating island in the lagoon's middle. About six feet square, it drifted randomly, pushed by wind and what small currents there were in the water, until it lurked right in the middle of my usual route. I would have to pass right by it, and it perturbed me.

Such places are havens for fish that use them for shelter from dive-bombers like kingfishers, and trawlers like terns and skimmers. It's no haven from caiman though. Enterprising caiman will investigate such places for snacks. I feared the black caiman would come over to have a look.

I swam even more slowly than usual as I approached the vegetation, only spurred on when my feet hit cold patches of water. For some reason I pictured doing a similar swim in northern Australia, or back in Botswana, and how terrifying it would be if a scaly head appeared beside me. I then moved to imagining the terrifying feeling of jaws clamping on a limb. I started swimming faster, powering past the makeshift island, the urge to have a little pee stronger than ever before, the fear of a candiru enough to keep it in. My swimming is all enthusiasm, no style, and now I was really churning the water, sure that something was stalking me, the mystery black caiman somewhere behind me, closing in.

I began to plan what I would do if I was grabbed. A friend had a smallish croc take his arm clean off once, not something I desired, but it was better than being grabbed by the torso and dragged down into the water and drowned. "Crocodilians have sensitive skin between their toes," a guiding instructor once told me in all seriousness. "And a good pinch there might make them release you." I couldn't imagine having the presence of mind to locate this particular patch of skin in such circumstances. In fact I thought it was far more likely I'd panic to death first. If, however, I did lose a limb, my board shorts had a drawstring, and I could rip that out and make a tourniquet, swimming to whatever bank was nearest, making sure to compensate for lopsidedness as I went.

There was a flaw in my plan, though. "Bloody piranhas," I thought. With that much blood in the water there was no way they would stick with their mainly vegetarian ways. No matter my desperation, I would not make any bank.

None of these ideas was comforting in the least. I hit my turn-around point, did not even pause, and started back, taking a wider route around the sinister vegetation, sure it had shifted its course to come closer, then just as sure I was being paranoid, forcing myself to straighten my route again and pass the bloody thing.

Suddenly some nostrils appeared beside me and kept pace. I made a sobbing noise, sure I'd willed my fear into existence; a panicky flurry from my legs sent ripples over the nose and made it disappear, which was even worse than being able to see it.

My mind took a moment to process what I had seen, busy as it was reverting to that of a scared child. Then I realized that the nostrils had been tiny and closely spaced—a reptile to be sure, but no caiman. The nostrils reappeared, then a whole head belonging to a terrapin. "Tortoises live on land and have little round feet like elephants," I have explained to many a tourist. "Turtles live in the ocean and have flippers. Terrapins live in freshwater and have webbed feet." I irrationally blamed this one for the terror it had caused me, then immediately changed my mind. Perhaps it would act as bait for anything larger. It tracked with me a while, and with my focus on it rather than the bogey caiman, I was able to enjoy my swim once more, not even flinching too much or squealing when submerged vegetation brushed my leg.

Despite my fears, I went back into the lagoon day after day, plunging off the board, out and back, then out and back again, eventually building to three times across—no great achievement but after a year on the road it was refreshing to not feel like a piece of cheese.

During my last few days at Sacha, the friends who had facilitated my stay, Pete and Renee, came in to visit the camp and get some photos for their portfolios. As I pointed out a place where the pygmy marmosets crossed a path each day, one of them with a thumb-size baby with an old man's face, I announced that I was off for my daily swim.

"How far do you go?" Pete asked.

"Three times across and back," I answered, expecting perhaps some admiration, not really factoring in that it was not all that far.

"I wouldn't," Pete said simply. Pete has lived in Ecuador for twenty-five years and traveled the world photographing animals, getting the very first images of certain species in the wild, so when it comes to wildlife he's someone to listen to.

So I didn't listen, that day or for the rest of my stay, and carried on with my swim.

Pete and Renee stayed on when I left, but e-mailed me a few days later.

"Remember that story we told you about the Peruvian primate researcher?" they wrote. I did.

He had disappeared while taking what was, for him, a regular swim just like mine, somewhere in the Manu National Park. No trace had been found, not a scrap of flesh, not a piece of swimwear. If a caiman had grabbed him, there would have been some grisly evidence, same if he had somehow been nabbed from the shore by a jaguar; and if he had merely drowned, it would become evident over time when his body appeared. There was only one reasonable suspect.

"Well, the day after you left," the e-mail continued, "an anaconda was coiled right at the place you used to turn around. We couldn't see how long it was because it was piled up, but one section was as thick as a thigh. That could easily take a man."

"Bugger," I thought. "An anaconda. Didn't think of that one."

20

A Month of Monkeys, a Night of Darkness

It was all the monkeys' fault.

And the birds.

Or maybe mine.

Not only did Sacha have six hundred birds species in its area, it also held eight species of monkey. This amazed me—the whole southern African region holds only two species of monkey, and Sacha is an island of only a few acres, surrounded by oil interests and illegal forestry and poaching. Yet squirrel monkeys, black-mantled tamarins, rare night monkeys, and the incredibly cute pygmy marmosets resided within the lodge's grounds, with other shier species staying farther out in the jungle.

During my month at Sacha I set myself the challenge of seeing all eight species of monkey. In three weeks, with some effort, I'd seen seven. So I was unusually delighted when fruit fell on me while I was out on a trail one day, and the fruit flinger turned out to be a dusky titi, the eighth species I'd wanted to see.

Soon after the dusky titi and its family had scampered off, I became distracted by a mixed flock of birds moving through the jungle undergrowth. Next thing I knew I was starting to tick bird species off my list as well. My progress on the trail was slow, but only because I was so enthralled by the bounty it held. All the while there was something else I should have been paying attention to.

I had reached the point of being able to walk the trails without a guide and had somehow mastered the art of seeing monkeys and discriminating between branches that were moving because of a breeze and branches moving due to the weight of an animal. But the real trick is to see the monkeys without them seeing you. So after the titis had moved on and the birds had dispersed, I was very proud when I managed to hide against a tree trunk before some howler monkeys saw me.

I'd imagined the jungle in Sacha would be a place of thick, impenetrable vegetation, a green barrier filled with snakes and hairy tarantulas everywhere, with plenty of cover to make it easy for me to view wildlife. But real rain forest has such a closed canopy that less than 10 percent of light gets through, so not much grows in the understory at all, and few snakes or spiders perturb those who are not in their fan club. Even cover at Sacha wasn't this thick, but still it wasn't what I had imagined, and there wasn't much place for me to hide. The howler monkeys carried on and then settled in the tree above me for the night. I stayed motionless for a while, then began to wonder if I was jungle savvy enough to sneak away without disturbing them.

All at once the male made a noise like an engine firing up.

Soon the whole family (of which there were five) joined in the howling, and I was subjected to the ear-rattling cacophony of the world's loudest animals, an ear bruising greater than any rock concert. Using binoculars I focused on the male's throat pouch, which was ballooning with each long breath. The little ones did their best to imitate their dad, their cheeks stretching close to bursting. It was the second best thing I'd ever heard, after a wild lion's roar up-close, and I was transfixed—so transfixed in fact that I didn't grasp that the monkeys were shouting at the dusk and it was about to get dark. Day length is constant at the equator, and there was no reason I should have been surprised that the sun set at six, just as it did every night.

Bugger, I thought. It was already beyond dim at tree level, and what little light was left was blocked by foliage. I needed to decide whether to backtrack to the lodge as quickly as possible or carry on ahead in a direction I was pretty sure would take me to the lodge. Many of the forest trails at Sacha are like anacondas at an orgy, twisting and crossing each other with no discernible pattern, which made doubling back the sensible thing to do.

So I didn't.

Instead I found the trail looped away from where I wanted it to and became harder to make out in the dimming light. Sadly, my outdoor skills didn't extend to making a flashlight out of the local resources, which were mainly decaying leaves and mosquitoes—lots of them. Fallen leaves in the jungle acted as cups and made perfect breeding ground for bloodsuckers. I plunged ahead, inhaling a mosquito or six and coughing enough to make me panic a little. Or maybe the panic was just because I knew I'd been stupid.

If I'd been lost in the jungle at dusk in Africa, all I could have done was climb a tree and hope to be found by people before a leopard found me. Here at least I didn't have to worry about cats, since pumas—though ubiquitous in many parts of South America—had not been recorded at Sacha. And I was more likely to be impregnated by a llama than get lucky and see a jaguar.

The sensible thing to do was sit tight, wait, and see if any-one noticed my absence, though even if they did they'd have no idea where to begin looking for me. My second option was to cover myself with my poncho and some insect repellent and wait for morning, then backtrack.

So I didn't.

I became very aware of the smells of decaying leaves, the screeching of insects, and the low thrum of some unknown toad or frog. Then after a while I realized the low thrum was actu-ally the Lodge's generator, so maybe it wasn't so far away after all. Unfortunately, just as the canopy swallows light, the forest absorbs sound.

By this stage it was so dark in the forest I could barely see, but I was still on some sort of trail and tried to follow it. My wonky hearing has often led me in the wrong direction—and this appeared to be the case now, because the sound of the generator seemed to be getting quieter. I didn't know if the trail would continue in the right direction. And if it diverted, I wasn't sure whether I should carry on.

I lost the option of choosing to be an idiot and had it thrust upon me. The villain was a dastardly root that wrapped around my boot and tripped me. I swiveled in the air, landing arched over my pack and instinctively clutching my binoculars high and safe. I scrambled back up quickly, worried about army ants, and any other thing that might want to crawl on and bite me, then realized I'd lost all sense of direction again. Shaking damp leaves from my hair, I looked around for the trail but couldn't even see my feet. I was now immersed in a darkness so complete it was unlike any-thing I'd ever experienced.

Cursing myself for not replacing a blown bulb in my Maglite, I slowly and cautiously made my way forward, hands outstretched, breath so ragged it sometimes drowned out the noise I was trying to follow.

Then I saw a light. It was red and pulsed as I moved, as if trying to signal me through the foliage. Convinced it was the lodge, obscured by swaying leaves, I slid my feet in its direction. But it was now to my left, so I changed course, and it did too, baffling me momentarily until it winked at me then zoomed straight up. *Red fireflies?* I wondered. The Amazon is the clear winner when it comes to insects, which are all brighter, bigger, and/or louder than their equivalents in other parts of the world—or they are just so strange they appear to be the result of some insane dream. I pushed ahead again, my palms forward, my legs moving in a blind zombie shuffle.

After a while my hands brushed something soft and furry. I flinched back, stumbling again, and bounced off a tree. Suddenly I felt claws clutching me from all sides, flailing, terrified. Something was biting me, something was tearing at me.

Despite my fear, I forced myself to stay still and think rationally. The soft material was most likely balsa fluff, or drifting cotton from a kapok tree, though I was sure it was a big, ugly, hairy tarantula, like a Russian's knuckles going for a walk. The teeth and claws were no more than thorny vines, and I picked my way out, more than ever thinking it would be best to just give up. Instead I blundered on, the generator noise definitely louder, the path definitely gone.

"Go toward the light!" friends of faith have implored me over the years. And I finally did. Ahead of me a light pulsed, and at first I was sure it was just another firefly flaunting its freedom, but it came again, not blinking, just strobing in and out of my vision as the angle between it and the foliage changed. I made a beeline toward it, fumbling more, stumbling some, and finally tripping on a raised walkway, my hands out front now balled into fists lest there be spiders.

I got up, too thrilled to feel much pain, and shuffled into the lodge. I had no idea what time it was and just hoped a search party hadn't formed, which would have been mortifying.

I didn't pass any staff as I took a shortcut through the back of the lodge and dashed into my room. It was 7:45 p.m. What had felt like hours of being lost had been less than two, and I was only a few minutes late for dinner.

During the meal there was an announcement that Dan would be leading a night walk, and I thought it would probably be good to get right back on the tarantula, so to speak. I arrived before anyone else to the designated meeting place for the walk. A halogen lamp illuminated the spot, and bugs of hallucinogenic diversity dipped and dived at it, some bouncing off stunned into the grass below. When a lurid green cicada with bright red eyes did just this, I reached down to grab it and take a closer look. The shadow my arm cast swelled and lengthened, as if a giant was probing the earth; nearby a second shadow of a twig made a dark stripe on the lawn close beside it.

That twig looks a bit like a snake, I thought just before said object flicked a forked tongue toward my arm. My limb shot back with such speed it may have made a sonic pop, and Dan arrived to find me sprawled on the deck to get a closer look at what he quickly identified as a cat-eyed snake.

"Mostly harmless," he said. "Lucky it wasn't a fer-de-lance," he added, naming one of the region's most venomous and aggressive snakes. If it had been a fer-de-lance, or viper, or bushmaster, I would now be at serious risk of losing a limb, if not my life. No matter how well I had hidden from the howlers, clearly I had lost my jungle skills. There and then I decided that not only was I ill-suited to return to guiding, but that perhaps the jungle as a whole was not a great place for me to spend much more time. The sensible thing to do would be to leave.

So of course I didn't.

Nah, I thought. *Time to go deeper.* And with that idea began my most extreme journey yet.

21

Going Deeper

"Man, what happened to your face?" Tom asked me in his ever-jovial tone, his Southern U.S. accent still strong, even though he had lived in Ecuador for more than twenty years. Beside him stood a man I knew must be Otobo. Powerfully built, though little more than five feet tall, he had an undeniable intensity but greeted me warmly. We were in Coca, the same town I had used to access Sacha, but this time I would be heading farther into the Amazon basin and would visit Otobo's tribe, the Huaorani.

"Muggers," I said simply. "Three of them. And I'd had enough to drink to think it was a good idea to fight back. Probably wasn't," I finished, indicating the black eye, abraded neck, and lumped lip that adorned my face. There was also a gash on my head where one assailant had broken a beer bottle. It was still bleeding slightly, releasing glass shards once a day or so.

Tom translated all this into Spanish for Otobo, a little loosely and more than a little generous about my prowess. Otobo nodded at me, seemingly impressed at my warrior spirit. Perhaps my misshapen nose (a product of genetics, not fighting) gave the impression that I fought a lot. And lost often.

"All three ran from me," I carried on, but some fondness for honesty made me add, "admittedly by then they had twenty dollars and a credit card." Tom again translated, but even with my limited Spanish I could tell he was once again praising my fighting abilities. It hadn't been much of a brawl—my style is less martial arts and more crazed raccoon—but it had reminded me that not everyone I met on my travels would be friendly.

The Huaorani also had a reputation for unfriendliness. The tribe only became aware of the outside world—and the world of them—in the late 1950s. Their name translates to mean "the people," as they consider outsiders of any ethnic group to be something else, usually *cowode,* a term that loosely means "cannibal." From the 1950s to today they have been the victims of missionary attention and ruthless oil companies (sometimes both) working in tandem to drive them from their land. Otobo had met Tom and his wife Mariela when they helped a neighboring tribe, the Kichwa, set up an ecotourism operation of their own. Even though his family had dabbled in working for the oil companies and some had strayed to cities, Otobo thought that allowing others to see how and where his people lived would be a way to preserve his culture and make a living as well.

I was to spend three weeks with him, three weeks with no telephones, Internet service, newspapers, or modern distractions of any kind. They would be three of the most extraordinary weeks of my life.

Three English people had already been scheduled to travel with Tom and Otobo; I would piggyback on their trip and then stay with the Huaorani for two weeks after they left. I'd just returned from a month-long visit with Lisa in England

and had lost any tan I might have had. The six of us set off in an open-backed truck with bench seats from Coca along the harshly named Via Auca (literally, "the road of savages") built by Texaco, indicating the antipathy of the Huaoroni's nearest neighbors. Along the way, other Huaorani Otobo knew flagged us down and we soon had a gathering of more than ten people. After several hours on a road well maintained by the oil companies, we came to a checkpoint that marked the entry to Yasuni National Park, where military officials checked our health papers and stamped us in as if we were leaving Ecuador and entering a whole new country. In the minds of the Huaorani, of course we were. This was their land.

After the checkpoint came long hours in a motorized canoe. Otobo was very proud of his long river craft made of fiberglass. We saw fewer and fewer signs of development, then no sign of humanity at all.

We camped in dome tents by the river that night, and Otobo's traveling companions introduced themselves to us, some in Spanish that Tom translated, others in their native language of *Huao* (pronounced wow). Everyone's introduction was brief, except for the guy who rambled on forever about which village he was born in, where he grew up, and innumerable other details. "I don't like flies," he even said at one point. Tom just let him go on, afterward explaining that he had a reputation for aggression.

Then we were all given Huaorani names, a process that the five of them all consulted over. Mine was *Ayare*, because I reminded them of someone named that who was tall. Most Huaorani are barely above five feet, so, I *am* tall in their part of the world, though I imagined the Minke laughing at that idea. *Ayare* was also known as a flirt, I was told, and I am sure that with my black eye I must have seemed a real catch.

That night an owl called throughout the evening, a mournful and sleep-defying call. The next day when we asked Otobo what it was he said, "A really big one. Bigger than an eagle. Bigger than a man even."

Later we actually found the owl in the trees. It was maybe a foot or so in size, but from below it looked huge. Therefore to the Huaorani it was.

I soon realized why traditionally the Huaorani don't wear clothes. It rains furiously at least once a day—and this was the dry season. In the wet season it rains twice a day. Clothes get soaked and have no time to dry before the next drenching, creating a perfect environment for fungus and parasites. It is only in the open spaces above the river that any light can penetrate, so Otobo steered exactly midriver, swerving only for stumps and the occasional river dolphin.

We camped another night and spent another full day puttering downriver before finally reaching Otobo's village, a three-building affair. One building housed Otobo, his wife, and their three children; another, only a few hundred yards away, was home to his parents, their pet macaw, several dogs, and a spider monkey who hissed his intent to bite at any approach. The third building was for Otobo's brothers, who passed through occasionally.

The English tourists were bird-watchers, which suited me fine. Bird-watchers usually see more animals than anyone else, as they are attuned to the smallest movements and differences in color and know how to sit patiently and quietly. So we spent our first full day out of the canoe at a salt lick, watching rainbow streams of parrots come to eat the nutrient-rich clay that counters various toxins in their food.

"So, you going to get naked?" Tom asked me.

"Sure," I replied. "But . . . they are all in their seventies," I indicated the English, "I don't imagine they want to see me nude, nor me them." One of the guides at Sacha who had some knowledge of the Huaorani had told me that they would never trust me until I was naked, as that was the only way they would know I wasn't hiding anything.

"The reason I asked is that Omagewe," Tom indicated Otobo's father, a miniscule but muscled man somewhere in his sixties, "was laughing earlier and saying you should take your pants off."

"Really? I had no idea we'd become so close already."

Tom just laughed. I was bathing in the chocolate milk–colored waters of the River Coanaco. There *were* candirus here, and caiman, stingrays, and hidden stumps. I also had a reason to fear piranha with my head still bleeding. I was treating it with nothing but pawpaw ointment.

By Christmas Day the wound was beginning to heal, so apparently it was time I scored another injury. Christmas means little to me, and even less to the Huaorani, but they prepped a smoked chicken for us in an effort to honor the holiday, and we had a thoroughly pleasant day that had nothing to do with the calendar. I bird-watched, poked around in the jungle, and paddled in a borrowed canoe with Omagewe laughing at me from the bank. I saw an ornate hawk eagle's nest and heard the scurrying of jungle animals around me. I wanted to live like this for as long as I could, but reality insisted I could not. In between Sacha and this trip I had visited Lisa in London and had met up with several of my old safari friends who had been attending a travel trade show. They offered me a very intriguing job that involved travel—lots of it—and the chance to do some good, as the company is not really a business at all but a conservation organization disguised as one. But I still hadn't made a decision.

Disaster struck that night as I made my way into my small tent. A searing pain hit my hand as I undid the zipper, and I immediately turned ashen.

"Mariela! Tom!" Otobo's brother, Bartolo, shouted. "Peter's been bitten by a snake!"

Bartolo was wrong. It was a Konga ant. Unfortunately these are the size of a bullet and pack as much ill intent. Some people who are bitten by one have fevers lasting days. I took some painkillers, writhed a while, sure I would have no sleep that night, but then I fell deeply asleep.

No fever had emerged the next day, a welcome gift as December 26 is my birthday. Only Otobo, who has spent more time with outsiders than many Huaorani, knew the concept; to the Huaorani the notion of a birthday makes no sense. They have no record of when they were born, because to them it simply does not matter. Any day can be special in the jungle, whether it brings food, a baby, or a pleasant reunion with family.

I saw several new birds, and Mariela treated me to a cake made from two stacked pancakes slathered with Nutella. And I met Otobo's father-in-law, a smiling older fellow with Bon Jovi hair, who stood about five feet, one inch. Together with Omagewe (Otobo's father), he chanted a history to us. It basically involved all the people they had killed—Otobo's father-in-law managed five in a war with *petroleros* (oil workers) back in the 1970s.

Later that evening I saw a spectacular hummingbird the size of a starling, with tail streamers that curved and crossed each other, covered in iridescent red plumage. The fiery topaz was very high on my wish list, and it filled me with a certain optimism. Everything felt like it was getting closer. A jaguar must be nearby. The Huaorani were right—any day could be a special one in the jungle.

22

Tigre! Tigre!

On December 27 we spent four hours in the canoe to go to a village called Bameno. In the 1970s this was an oil exploration camp, but the Huaorani drove the *petroleros* out (with spears) and took over the property to stop them from returning, thereby inheriting a gravel airstrip that they have maintained in rough form to this day. As soon as the English tourists left, I got naked.

■ ■

As I mentioned, it is customary among the Huaorani to go naked. The Huaorani accessorize their look with a string; the men tuck their genitals into it to keep from being snagged while climbing trees after food; the women use it to hold a leaf in place for modesty's sake. Otobo's grandfather, Quempere, added a necklace of red and blue plastic beads to his ensemble that had among them alphabet beads. Omagewe wore shorts most days, but in his home or while hunting he went naked save the string. One day, much to my surprise, he strolled over wearing underpants so large he had to tuck them into his string and an extralarge lurid green T-shirt emblazoned with Abercrombie and Fitch. It was, of course, a cheap

Chinese knockoff. I often found it amusing when some of the Huaorani unconsciously mimicked young male Westerners by wearing their shorts (when they wore them) very low. They wore them so low, in fact, that it was obvious they weren't wearing underpants.

While we're on the subject of fashion, the Huaorani men also sported some fine hairdos. Otobo's father-in-law had stepped straight off the cover of a Bon Jovi album. Quempere wore his locks in a traditional cut, long with straight bangs stopping just above his eyebrows, trimmed regularly with sharpened mollusk shells. Otobo had a fine mullet, and I saw a child in Bameno who somehow maintained a perfect Elvis pompadour.

■ ■

And so it was in full Huaorani regalia—nothing but a string—that we met the whole village before making our way to the house of Quempere, the jaguar shaman. He gave me the heartening news that he would send the spirit of a jaguar to the river's edge, or somewhere in the forest where I would see it.

Then, being me, I dove into the Cononaco River, which flows past the village, and swam a little more than half a mile. Nakedness caused me a certain delirium, and I ignored the dangers of caiman, piranhas, and candiru.

That night we camped downstream from the river, and several of the village elders accompanied us. There were two new tourists, a bit more culturally adventurous than the English had been, and I was feeling moldy from constantly wearing damp clothes. Allan, an aspiring television host, and his cameraman, Fernando, didn't seem fazed by my nudity, or theirs. They shared my delight in the playful nature of the Huaorani men, including Otobo's father, who I increasingly thought of as the Amazing Omagewe. Despite being somewhere in his sixties, he climbed trees as if they were ladders, laughing all the while as I watched in amazement below. I wanted to join in but feared abrading parts of my body that were sunburned for the very first time.

That night we took a cruise in the canoe to look for caiman. I had a hefty Maglite in the bow and eventually found a reasonably size caiman on a bank (Marcello would have undoubtedly called it "Huge!"). On the way back I concentrated the light on the banks rather than the water, and not far from our camp I hit eye shine on the far bank.

"*Tigre!*" shouted Otobo.

The Spanish make no linguistic distinction between the large spotted cat they encounter in South America and the huge striped one in Asia.

But as I shone the light out of the cat's eyes and onto its body, it was apparent this was wasn't a jaguar. It was an ocelot. I felt momentarily deflated, until I realized that this was the first wildcat I'd seen in South America, even if it wasn't a jaguar. More would come, surely.

■ ■

But instead of a cat, a fever came to me that night. Perhaps it was a delayed reaction to the ant bite, or maybe some tropical parasite. But whatever it was, I had a fitful night with a fever that made me shake against the thin sheet I used as a cover. Tom had suffered Dengue fever the year before and said my symptoms mirrored that disease, something that would require an evacuation to some distant hospital. But in the morning I felt well again, and I joined Omagewe on a search for Otobo's grandfather. Quempere, Omagewe's father-in-law, had wandered off into the forest after a vision. He was considered one of the most powerful shamans in the entire Huaorani tribe and frequently pursued objects only he could see. There were some concerns among Otobo's family that Quempere was becoming senile, and so finding him was a priority.

"Quempere! Woo hoo!" Omagewe shouted, then laughed. "Quempere!"

I joined in, which for some reason was even funnier, and all four feet, ten inches of Omagewe's frame doubled over with laughter. Omagewe spoke only Huao, and I had only learned a word or two, but we discovered that so much communication can be done without language.

We eventually found Quempere back at the canoe, baffled at our concern, using a palm frond as an umbrella against the rain, which was once more lashing down in diagonal streaks so thick it was blinding. Omagewe's visible relief dispelled any thought I might have had that he found the search hilarious only because he didn't care about its outcome. The Huaorani live in the now, and until there was real reason, he wasn't going to be worried about the future. He had obviously been confident we would find Quempere and was so innately happy and optimistic that he could enjoy the search.

Back at the campsite we gathered at the fire. Those of us who were naked stood in a communal huddle, laughing at each other's chattering teeth.

The next night my fever came back and slow roasted me until it broke, and rivers of sweat soaked my skin. After finally falling asleep, I was woken by a horrific wailing. As I lay awake, I immediately thought of the Tagaeri and the Taromanane, the region's two tribes who have no contact at all with the outside world. Their interactions with the Huaorani were at times very violent. The Tagaeri are close relatives of the Huaorani, but Otobo's family swear the Taromanane are not.

Some years ago the Huaorani killed twenty-three Tagaeri in revenge for deaths in their community, even though it turned out the Tagaeri were not responsible. The Huaorani believe that someone is responsible for every death, be it from illness, old age, or an attack, and so all deaths must be avenged. It doesn't seem workable long-term to behave in such a way, and the policy is dying out. We had met the niece of the man who organized the slaughter, and she said she would never kill anyone but an oil worker.

The Taromanane are altogether different from the Tagaeri. Not long before our visit, Omagewe went hunting for several days and left his wife alone at their hut. One night she came outside and saw a group of Taromanane at the edge of their field. According to her they were tall and pale—"As tall and white as you," she said, pointing at me. When they spoke she couldn't understand them, but she called them her brothers and said they should take what they wanted from the field, and then she went back inside and waited, hoping not to be speared.

Otobo was a natural guide. He flipped a switch between the demands of the older bird-watchers and Fernando and Allan, who were more culturally intrigued. He anticipated their needs as if he had attended the finest tourism management school.

Omagewe was a master of the forest, a skillful hunter, who was able to turn invisible whenever he wanted. He may have been the most dangerous man I've ever known, with a significant body count of *petroleros* and illegal loggers to his name. Yet his constant laughter made it almost impossible for me to imagine him as a spear-wielding killer.

Then there was Penti. Most Huaorani I met were stocky, but Penti was slender and sported a natty Clark Gable moustache. For more than twenty years he fought to protect his home from oil companies and was knowledgeable about the challenges the Huaorani faced.

Twice in the past oil companies had been allowed to extract oil from within the national park, and it was disastrous both times. Texaco spilled more oil in the Ecuadorian Amazon than the *Exxon Valdez* did in Alaska, and the roads that were built to facilitate the extraction acted like a cancer in the forest, spreading the poison of illegal logging, poaching, and colonists who moved in. All this encroachment was dividing up once-pristine blocks of wilderness and the homeland of the Huaorani territory.

■ ■

"Did I scream out last night?" Fernando asked back in the canoe. "I think I was having a nightmare."

The very air felt hallucinogenic, or maybe it was just my fever, but I was not surprised that people have such dreams in the jungle. Fernando, as well as Tom, Mariela, and Allan, was at the end of his Huaorani visit. We were canoeing to Bameno, from which they would fly out while I stayed on for another two weeks away from the *cowodes*. My fever was back and the sunlight felt like spears to my eyes. As soon as we made it to Bameno, I curled into a hammock to have my own nightmares at a house made of palm poles and thatched with leaves that Otobo kept there,

I was woken by a squawking macaw that wandered in, screeched at me several times, then ambled back out. Village life puttered all around. Some people cooked, some snoozed, and some lazily played a soccer game. The heat was stifling. People in various states of dress walked in and out of the house, some shaking me awake to ask questions like: "In the United States, how many wives do you have?" (It didn't matter how many times I said I was Australian; all *cowodes* were from America.) Chickens came in and out as freely as the people.

"I have only one," I said, because they also made no distinction between a wife and girlfriend, "but she is in England." Considering how often I make faux pas in my own language, I was quite nervous that I might have just said, "Why, yes, sir, I would very much like to have congress with your chicken!" but apparently they had understood my meaning.

"Huh," they scoffed. "You should get more."

Even Otobo said he wanted more than one wife but was too busy with his business. Huaorani women don't outnumber men as they once did, perhaps because of the decrease in violence between tribes. Bameno, with maybe fifty inhabitants, was far busier than Otobo's little spot upriver, which normally only had five or six inhabitants before his wife arrived with their two daughters and newborn son. "My son has six fingers on each hand!" Otobo let me know proudly, "and six toes, too!"

Everyone was related in some way among the Huaorani, which might have accounted for the occasional surfeit of fingers and toes. The ethnic Huaorani only number about two thousand individuals, as they have done for hundreds if not thousands of years.

23

Parrots, Prayers, and the End of a Year

On the last day of 2010 I awoke to see the jaguar shaman peering at me through a gap in the wall as I lay in my hammock.

"*Waponi* Quempere," I said, using the very useful Huao word *waponi,* which means "hello," "good-bye," and "good." Then I added, *"Ibanoimi?"* which means "How are you?" He just laughed and sat beside me on the hammock, his wife following close by. With clawed hands he studied my hair, teeth, and palms, before clapping my hands together and laughing heartily once more. Quempere was probably about eighty. His wife looked a sprightly sixty.

The same macaw from the day before walked in and screeched a few words. *Great,* I thought, *even a bloody parrot speaks more Huao than me.*

Throughout my stay I was keeping a diary for Lisa, who I sorely missed, trying to make up for our lack of contact during my time with the Huaorani. As I sat to write on the last day of 2010, I realized that I had no idea what day of the week it was, nor did I care. The Huaorani jabbed fingers at my notebook as I wrote. Only the youngest could read at all, and then in Spanish, but all seemed fascinated by the marks I made on the page. It would have seemed a breach of privacy anywhere else, but in this off-kilter world, it was not at all unpleasant or invasive to have Quempere and his extended clan all watching me and my scratchings at the page.

■ ■

That afternoon we made our way back to Otobo's home by canoe in roughly four hours. After a short break we traveled another hour to an even smaller village that was the home of Otobo's cook, who had chosen as his Western name the fitting moniker of Conan. I was surprised to discover that a man I had met the first night was Conan's brother, who went by Eduardo. He had been the one who told his entire life story and spoken to me of the happiness he'd found in Jesus with the help of some missionaries, but had struck me as less happy than any Huaorani I'd met. But on our second meeting I decided that even if he wasn't as happy as the others, he was still very generous, patient, and gentle despite my obvious ineptitude as he taught me spear throwing, while his wife cooked us manioc and fish served on a palm leaf and eaten with the fingers.

My stomach was queasy or I would not have hesitated over the food, which we ate after communally rinsing our hands in tea-colored water, but I smiled and ate it anyway. Here in the jungle Eduardo seemed thoroughly content in a way I never could have imagined a year before while locked in my old life. He pointed out Monk Sakis nearby, a beautiful, woolly coated species of monkey I'd only seen once before. He was Huaorani, just more exposed to the outside world than the others, but he had the generosity common to them all. Maybe this is what all Huaorani would become as the world closed in on them—but maybe not.

We stopped at Otobo's place after our visit with Conan and Eduardo, and I helped unload the boat by hauling seats, tanks of water, and gas cylinders up a muddy slope. Suddenly everything wavered and I briefly fainted, something I had never done before. It seemed to be a symptom of the illness that was plaguing me every night but abated during the day. I was pretty sure it wasn't Dengue, but I didn't know what it was.

Later I went to bathe in the river, wearing a bathing suit this time as a precaution against candiru. Most of the embankments by the river were muddy, and with any foot traffic they quickly turn into the consistency of chocolate mousse. The trail led to Otobo's "beach," a sandy patch that only turned muddy once you were ankle-deep, meaning with some tricky foot shaking you could emerge clean.

On the trail a column of army ants, maybe twenty wide, swarmed laterally across my path in a hypnotic stripe of constant movement. I hopped over them. Army ants are so feared that even a jaguar will move out of their way. Roughly half an inch long and menacingly black, they are one of the Amazon's more potent animals. When they fan out in a swarm to forage, they can devour absolutely everything in their way. There were stories of chickens trapped in coops that were stripped to the bone in minutes by these insects.

The column of ants doubled back onto the path. I hopped over them again, then the column turned perpendicularly. I straddled each side of it, then it split into two columns, then more again, and I found myself surrounded. Glancing behind me I saw that the trail back to the village was now covered, and with no time to think I launched into a run, my tender feet seeking the places with the fewest ants. But the first bites began immediately and caused excruciating pain in both feet. I broke into a sprint, not caring what I trod on.

The sprint was probably a bigger mistake than not turning back and trying my luck that way. I felt another faint coming on. Falling and blacking out here would leave me so covered in bites the situation might be fatal. *Don't let me die this way,* I thought briefly, recalling stories of elderly people killed by army ants because they couldn't move fast enough.

I staggered to the water and flopped in, only to find that the bites had paralyzed my feet to a degree but had not deadened the pain receptors. My agony flared anew. It might have been only a fifty-yard swim to the nearest ant-free bank, but it would not be easy (or wise) to swim such a distance with paralyzed legs and fainting spells. But there was no way in hell I was walking back.

24

Chasing a Jaguar

It was my first booze-free New Year's Eve in more than a hundred years, and I was in bed right around nightfall. I spent another feverish night but woke in the morning feeling the best I had in some time. So I found a beautiful wooden canoe that was filled with water and mud, bailed it out, and spent several idyllic hours paddling up the small river that flanks one side of Boanamo before it joins the murky Coanaco.

I saw my first ever Jesus lizard that morning. It was something straight out of a cartoon when it reared onto its back legs and whirred them across the top of the water until it reached safety on the other side. I spent the rest of the day with Omagewe and his wife, who decided to make me some armbands out of palm cotton and strands of Omagewe's hair that he had crudely hacked off with a knife. She built a loom from kindling-size branches and the tough aerial roots that the Huaorani use for twine, then threaded the cotton round and through until it made a tight weave.

While she worked, Omagewe pantomimed the morning's hunt, during which he'd speared a peccary, a piglike mammal about half his size. He laughed as always, chortling hardest at the part where he fell from a tree and the peccary slashed his ankle with its tusk. The Huaorani seemed to find comedy in everything.

The next day, from what I could determine in the broken Spanish Otobo and I spoke to each other, I was going to be sent off deeper into the jungle and would sleep near one of the natural salt licks, waking as often as I could in the hope that a jaguar would be using it. I had lost track of the days of the week, but keeping a diary made me constantly aware that the date of my departure from the jungle and the continent was stalking, getting closer, and about to clamp down on me.

Inspired by my time with the Huaorani and a feeling I had to actively protect wild places, I'd decided to take the job, and once I left the Huaorani I'd be heading out of South America after eighteen months there. I wanted the most from the last few days. I wanted a jaguar.

I waited to see if Otobo had further plans. He asked me in Spanish, "Is it the first today?"

"No. *Esta el segundo*," I replied.

He didn't seem taken aback or surprised to be wrong about the date. Huao numbers only go as high as twenty. After that they simply use the words *nange* ("a lot") and *baco* ("many"). Even the numbers they do use are complicated to say—their counting goes one, two, two and one, two and two, five, five and one, and so on. So for example to tell someone I was thirty-six I would say, "*Bototepenpoga go tepenpoga go tepenpoga go emempoke go arokai.*" Or I could simply say *baco*.

This is probably why most Huaorani will tell you some patently absurd figure when you ask how old anything is. When I asked Quempere's age, I was told "more than one hundred" and "somewhere near sixty," and one youngster gravely told me that Otobo was "probably more than twenty," clearly impressed at such longevity. "He's probably in his eighties," Tom had said, "just based on the age of his children and their children."

Otobo straddles both the world of the Huaorani and the world outside and does it well—because of this he is wealthy by his community's standards, but this doesn't give him particular status here. Food is valued, treasured even, but not refrigerated, so it's not saved. When there is abundance, the people gorge. Traditional food, which I began eating when the food we'd brought from Coca ran out, included *paca* (a rodent slightly larger than a rabbit), a type of caterpillar, and eventually the peccary that had gored Omagewe.

I was glad to partake of these things, but other low stocks were a bigger problem. My camera battery died, and my sunscreen ran out soon after. The first was merely sad, the other dangerous, considering my new penchant for bare-assed exploration. The Huoarani, of course, laughed at me, as every inch of me was burned. I just pointed at my pink bits and laughed back.

■ ■

The next morning I didn't go to the salt lick. Plans were as flexible as time and numbers here, which I'd learned to consider as liberating, not frustrating. Instead Omagewe took me for a jungle walk. There is a rhythm to jungle walking. It is less frantic than a city walker's pace, less harried, but somehow feels faster, more elegant, a glide compared to a thump. A jungle walker's feet must be in tune with his eyes, the same eyes that watch the canopy for prey or danger, and yet can pick out the quietest and most efficient way of placing each limb. It requires the most intense concentration but is conversely relaxing—a mobile meditation. Both exhilarating and soothing, it may be our species' oldest and finest art.

I'm crap at it.

Twigs snap under my feet, branches rustle as my arms brush against them, and my permanent toothy display of joy must act like a signal ("Look! Over there! It's a human idiot! Hide quick!") to my quarry.

Making it worse was that I had decided on boots for the trip, no doubt a fetching complement to my string, but necessary as my baby-soft feet left me hopping, cursing, and stumbling in blind pain whenever I tried walking without them—surely a spearable offense should I chase food away.

For Omagewe, this jungle was a book he had read so often that every page was familiar. In Africa I may have advanced to a Dr. Seuss level of proficiency; here I didn't even know the alphabet. Omagewe regaled me today with long tales in Huao peppered with some Spanish words he has just learned for *hot water, jaguar, head* and *monkey,* chuckling as he acted out hunts, mainly of peccaries, but for all I know he may have slipped in a tale or two about picking off oil workers as well.

People who have visited the Huaorani told me about when they get "in the zone"—the moment when they become pure hunters. Omagewe entered that zone that day. He carried only a spear, so he could only hunt ground game, but while he was pointing out some woolly monkeys to me, they reacted as if he was fully equipped to discharge a dart from his blowgun and took off through the canopy. If he had managed to hit one with a poison-tipped palm arrow, he would have had to chase it, as the monkeys don't die immediately. So when these monkeys swung away, he shot off underneath them, and all of a sudden his four-foot-ten frame gave him an immense advantage. On a level track I am confident of my speed, but while Omagewe was swift, silent, and agile, I lumbered behind him in my flippety-flappety rubber boots feeling like a half-paralyzed elephant seal.

We came upon a fallen tree about a foot off the ground. Another tree had fallen on top of it, leaving a gap that was maybe two feet high, with lianas framing it on either side. Without breaking stride or losing sight of the monkeys, Omagewe jumped at the gap, tucking his legs and head in—a mighty ball of muscle with a spear protruding—and burst out the other side. I ran to it, briefly paused, and made the sensible decision to run around it, but by then had lost sight of Omagewe.

Some minutes later he came back, grinning sheepishly, spear still in hand, telling me with gestures and in Huao what had just happened, even though I had witnessed most of it. Then he told me again, this time with some monkey noises thrown in. He smiled at me and seemed to want a response.

"*Waponi,*" I said and, as expected, he laughed as if it was the best thing he'd ever heard.

When I finally made it out to the salt lick, I was completely alone, at least as far as human company went. Eight species of parrot, including three types of macaw, were squawking, cackling, chirping, and croaking around me, and I'd been visited by howler monkeys, spider monkeys, and a very large herd of white-lipped peccaries. Due to the peccaries' reputation for aggression,

I thought it best to entertain them from a perch a little way up in a tree. I spent more than an hour up there, which made me realize that after many encounters like that one, having a life with more hours treeborne as an adult than as a boy, was a fine thing, and I burst out laughing, scattering the peccaries briefly.

I would stay near the salt lick for two nights and three days. I had requested to spend this time alone not only to get a real feeling of the jungle, but to give Otobo's family a break from me. I had a little tent, plenty of water, my binoculars, some maize meal wrapped in vine leaves, and chocolate that Otobo miraculously produced, two flashlights, a spear Omagewe loaned me, and an imagination that just wouldn't stop taunting me with everything that could go wrong. It was exciting but also very frightening, so to soothe myself I started a list of things that could kill me:

1. Bushmaster/fer-de-lance/eyelash viper: These three snakes are all known to be here. The eyelash viper is moody because it has no hair, let alone lashes. Those are horns above its eyes—because it is the devil. I've never seen one, but that doesn't mean there isn't one in my tent. The fer-de-lance has a cross on the back of its head, like a pirate flag without the skull. I presume evolution is working on correcting that omission. Bushmasters . . . even Roy was afraid of these, and once after he saw one outside his cage he refused to come out for a whole day. They are pure evil with scales.

2. A jaguar: Now that would be deliciously ironic, wouldn't it?

3. Puma: It would book end my trip quite neatly to get bitten by a puma a week after arriving in South America, and a week before leaving, but I've never liked bookends.

4. Tagaeri: The amount of animals and large birds has increased dramatically in this area since Otobo's clan decided not to hunt here (a decision made in case he gets more tourists). Their abundance may attract Tagaeri, though hopefully not in the next two days. How likely that is nobody knows, as when discussing how many Tagaeri there are, even experts become Huaorani and grab a figure from the air. "One hundred! No, three hundred! One thousand!" Who knows? But I had my spear just in case. Oh goody.

5. Taromanane: They may not even exist according to some anthropologists (who may be funded by the oil companies who need figures showing there are fewer lives they will ruin, so have dubious credibility). But their nonexistence is no good to me if they aren't aware of it.

6. Peccaries: This option would be the most dignity stripping, but is still quite real. Should they catch me off guard and feel the need to avenge the deaths of their brethren at Omagewe's spear tip, I could be slashed and gored to death. Luckily they smell like a wrestler's armpit, so I should be able to detect them coming.

And with those pleasant thoughts I laid down. That night, for once, I actually hoped that I would have interrupted sleep and kept a watchful albeit bleary eye open for a jaguar and whatever else might come to my home sweet temporary home.

There were no incidents that night, which made me think my list quite silly. At first it was unnerving being so isolated, not in light, mind you, but once the darkness had rudely shoved the sun aside. Then I imagined footfalls (actually leaves falling from the trees) and heard breathing (it was my own), so I got up to face it all, grabbed the flashlight, and went for a night walk. I didn't see anything noteworthy, but calmed myself enough to drop into a deep sleep on my return, from which I awoke only a few times to check for jaguars or Taromanane.

Later on the second day I'd been sitting, concealed, for some time (hours? I had no way of knowing) as parrots inched their way closer to the lick, building the nerve to flutter in and get the nutrients they need from the clay. They were wary because predators are as aware as I was that this is a daily ritual, and any branch may hide a viper, every shadow some lethal cat.

They were very close when suddenly they erupted into a cacophony of squawks and a shower of guano. The sky filled with color as hundreds of birds wheeled away. Seconds later a hawk arrowed through with something red, green, and still twitching in its talons.

I don't like seeing any animals die, but this was so natural that it didn't make me flinch *Here it is!* I thought, feeling like I was seeing real life after too many sanitized experiences. *This is the real stuff! This is life!* I'm not a fan of conflict, but a complete absence of it can also dull humans to the pain of others, something I had felt in Sydney, where I even found myself complaining about the pettiest of life's inconveniences. Like nature itself, the Huaorani were only violent when the situation called for it. I once asked Otobo about this, and he said, "Huaorani don't like to fight at all! If there is a real problem with someone we just spear them."

On my second night at the salt lick I checked that my testicles were still present (they were), urged them to contribute some bravery, and went for a long nighttime walk. Again I saw nothing worth reporting, nor did anything occur, yet it remains to this day as one of the more frightening things I have ever done.

It was, most likely, also my last good chance to see a jaguar. Perhaps one would cross my path before Otobo took me back to Coca, but I doubted it.

25

The Honeymoon Period

Perspective is such a fickle thing. After three days alone in the jungle, Otobo's place felt like a bustling city. On my first day back at Otobo's village after an enormous meal that once again included paca, the clan piled into a canoe for the short paddle to Omagewe's hut, leaving me alone again. This was their life as they would live it whether I was there or not—some chores, some family time, very few clothes, and lots of laughter.

While I ate, I watched Otobo's daughter playing with what I thought at first was some sort of ragdoll before I realized it was the paca's baby, quite dead, but nevertheless she cooed at the rodent and even wrapped it in a blanket. Later, after one of the dogs had stolen it, she treated a bottle of cooking oil the same way, showing that certain instincts are global.

Everyone I have spoken to about the Huaorani believes they will be dragged into our modern world one way or another, and soon. And any number of groups want to adopt and "parent" them through the process, like they are children. But if you asked any parent I know what they want for their child they would say happiness. I have no idea what anyone could teach the Huaorani about that.

I came to think, perhaps naively, that the way the Huaorani live is like the early stages of a relationship when your love is perfect. The Huaorani seem content because the forest is abundant and they don't need more because they don't know what else is out there. Billions of us have moved passed that honeymoon stage, because we want too much and can never go back. Perhaps, as in a relationship when the first blush has faded, the trick is to find what you love and endure the rest. The more I thought about it, the more I realized what I needed to do was find what inspired me and filled me with joy, and use the rest of my time to do something that mattered to me.

If I could, I knew that I would give all of my clothes, the few other things I owned, even all that I knew of the world to be as shamelessly happy as Omagewe.

■■

My trip out of the Amazon jungle would involve another few days in the canoe. Since it hadn't rained for more than a week, and the river had dropped dramatically, navigating it would prove to be a challenge, as a whole new forest of stumps and snags emerged from the river bottom like broken teeth. Somehow, though, that just didn't seem to matter to the Huaorani. Otobo needed to take his youngest daughter back to Bameno, which was four hours downstream.

Ever keen to see what wildlife might be beside the river, I piled in too. This was a big mistake. Unlike the shaded smaller tributaries that crisscrossed around us, the Conanaco was broad, and open. Earlier I had been merely a bit pink. By the end of the day I was traffic-stopping red and throwing off so much heat that Otobo's wife placed wet clothes near me, saying I would dry them faster than the fire. It would have been merely uncomfortable and led to no more than a restless night in my hammock, but I had two more days in the canoe before hitting Coca, and the chance of some soothing lotion.

Fortunately for me, it began to rain hard and ceaselessly. Even the stoic Otobo took a T-shirt I offered him for some insulation. My three weeks had left me bearded, bedraggled, and bemolded, but that night in the jungle I knew I would miss it painfully. With Coca so close I began to think of the world, which had retreated in my mind, and craved a beer, a shower, meat not from a rodent, and contact with Lisa. Yet I kept an ear peeled, listening for a sound Marcello had taught me, a long rasp of a call that somewhere a jaguar hid from me. But all that night I lay sleepless, and no such sound came.

The next day we motored what seemed an anticlimactically short way and were back at the checkpoint, and soon after that I was on a bus back to Coca, the jungle around me scorched, slashed, gone.

I wanted to see a miracle: golden eyes peering from the forest as we broke camp or piled into the canoe, or a flash of fur as we motored along, but this is no fairy tale, and a jaguar did not appear.

If I had learned anything from the Huaorani it is that the trick of life is not to be content with what you have, but to be happy with what you do not. My trip was never really about jaguars anyway, or birds, or finding myself, or losing myself, or defying my age, but it was about seeking something wild and rare, not just in the jungle, but in me. Chasing the jaguar took me to so many places that I otherwise would have never seen if I'd owned a fridge or worked at a desk. Since it would stay hidden most of the time anyway, I decided to keep the Huaorani's string around my waist until it withered and fell off as a daily reminder of this philosophy.

I came to South America to find a jaguar, but I came away with so much more. I had found love, a country that made adversity somehow uplifiting, the scariest pet you could ever have, and that constant travel is exhausting. And that maybe, just maybe, it is okay to settle down—for a little while, anyway.

Of course I didn't find the jaguar, but that just means I have to keep looking.

Afterword

I often wish life was like a story; that you could go back and edit if it didn't work as it should, but I can't think of much that I would change about my eighteen months in South America. Overwhelmingly my memories are happy ones, but some are tinged with sadness.

Hollywood would have us believe that accidents happen in slow motion; a single well-said word can cure mental illness and grief; and that the greatest triumph of romance is for two people to overcome an obstacle to be together. But of course, accidents come at full, out-of-control speed; grief and illness are cured with time, if at all; and the hardest romantic endeavor is not just to get together, but to stay together. I didn't—couldn't—stay in London long, and the strain of too much time and distance meant that Lisa and I decided that our relationship could not reach across the space between continents. We remain friends, and I will forever be glad for her company through so much of the trip.

There's a balance I've found in my new life. I realize I don't need every day to hold something extraordinary. I just need the chance of it. I am now fully employed in a job I love—

with people I consider friends and on occasion even respect—traveling the world and quite enjoying the looks people give me when they see the dirty, frayed piece of string tied around my waist.

Peter Allison is the author of *Don't Look Behind You!* and *Whatever You Do, Don't Run* (both Lyons Press). His safaris have been featured in *Vogue* and *Condé Nast Traveller,* and he has appeared on television shows such as *Jack Hanna's Animal Adventures.* He does not live in any one place, but was last seen boarding a plane to Africa.

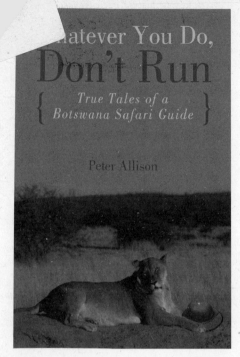

A hilarious, highly original collection of essays based on the Botswana truism: "Only food runs!"

Whatever You Do, Don't Run
True Tales of a Botswana Safari Guide
PETER ALLISON

....

978-0-7627-4565-4
$16.95 US/ $21.75 CAN
Paperback • 5 ¼ x 8 • 264 pp

"Allison's infectious enthusiasm for both the African bush and his job showing its wonders to tourists is readily apparent."
—*Booklist*

"His misadventures make *Whatever You Do, Don't Run* an absorbing read. . . . The material is rich, and Allison is a gifted storyteller. And the only thing stranger than African fiction is African truth."
—*National Geographic Adventure*

"After reading this entrancing memoir, an African safari may move to No. 1 on your travel wish list. The only catch is you'll want the author as your guide."
—*Chicago Sun-Times*

Globe Pequot Press
Guilford, Connecticut
www.GlobePequot.com

**To order, contact us
800.243.0495**